ALSO BY H MICHAEL ZAL

Panic Disorder: The Great Pretender
Da Capo Press: A member of the Perseus Book Group
ISBN 0-7382-0576-1

The Sandwich Generation: Caught Between Growing Children and Aging Parents
Da Capo Press: A member of the Perseus Book Group
ISBN 0-7382-0581-8

DANCING WITH MEDUSA
A LIFE IN PSYCHIATRY

A Memoir

H Michael Zal

authorHOUSE®

AuthorHouse™
1663 Liberty Drive
Bloomington, IN 47403
www.authorhouse.com
Phone: 1-800-839-8640

First published by AuthorHouse 3/17/2010

ISBN: 978-1-4490-7118-9 (e)
ISBN: 978-1-4490-7116-5 (sc)
ISBN: 978-1-4490-7117-2 (hc)

Library of Congress Control Number: 2010900749

Printed in the United States of America
Bloomington, Indiana

This book is printed on acid-free paper.

To My Parents

Evelyn & Frank Zal

They Loved Me In Their Own Way

The Best That They Could

Contents

FOREWORD

H Michael Zal, D.O., F.A.C.N., F.A.P.A., has written a captivating book that chronicles a period of experiences in his work in psychiatric medicine. More particularly, however, his piece presents a thirty-seven-year journey of heart that recounts a sincere human connection with a patient in treatment and the love of her family. Dr. Zal's narrative interprets not only the trials of a patient, but, moreover, the life lessons that both doctor and patient came to learn from each other. His memoir will evoke both laughter and tears; and ultimately, it will hearten the reader in the understanding that all people share some decidedly similar emotions.

Forty years in psychiatric practice could become a recipe for despair, but for Dr. Zal, it serves as a foundation for an inspiring tale of the interpersonal connection of the human soul as it is faced with the firm science of medicine.

For anyone who enjoys stories of the extraordinary, this memoir proves a reminder that hope, faith and human compassion are essential components in the practice of medicine. There is little doubt that the reader will glimpse a friend or a family member of his or her own in Zal's piece. If the adage - "he, who saves one life, saves the world entire" resonates at all, it is ever so evident here. Perhaps one of the greatest gifts one can give is the gift of "self" and this doctor does it often and wholeheartedly. Dr. Zal writes with compelling passion in telling a story of his patient's treatment - a head-to-head combat with mental and physical illness armed with the weapons of empathy and compassion. Dr. Zal made a difference by touching lives and he wrote this book to let readers know that in so doing, one is touched in return.

Dr. Zal's real-life *Patch Adams*-like tale resonates with those who believe that doctors should treat the patient, not the disease. There are many important points to be made in this piece about the dignity that all deserve when vulnerable and about the importance of human understanding in the direst of circumstances. In the end, Dr. Zal makes it clear that real treasure lies not in that which can be seen, but in that which cannot be seen.

Silvia M. Ferretti, D.O., Provost,
Senior Vice President and Dean of Academic Affairs,
Lake Erie College of Osteopathic Medicine

Author's Note/Acknowledgments

This is a story about Bella, whom I had the privilege to know over the course of thirty-seven years. We met at Haverford State Hospital in suburban Philadelphia in 1967. I was a 26-year-old green first-year resident in Psychiatry and she was a beautiful 20-year-old in the throws of a severe psychotic episode. Although I did not see her for treatment continuously, our lives intertwined professionally over the next many years. Although my life was quite different from Bella's, I was able to draw parallels from my childhood that allowed me to empathize with some of her feelings and life events.

As well as a personal history, this is also a memoir of discovery, which shows how my own early life and psychiatric training experiences brought me from the inexperienced, anxious, insecure psychiatric resident that I was in 1967 and helped me become a wiser, more empathetic and insightful therapist. It illustrates how I learned to balance personal angst, the biologic basis of psychiatric illness and the uniqueness of the individual patient into a precise therapeutic tool, which played out many times in my relationship with my patients through the years. This balancing act, illustrated through Bella's story, is the dance with medusa that has occupied the core of my life in psychiatry.

In each decade of my forty year psychiatric career, there have been sweeping advances in the field of psychopharmacology, changes in mental health laws and the ever-aggravating encroachments of managed care with the subsequent loss of physician control and a limiting of patient care. This has happened side by side with the gradual erosion of the role of the psychiatrist and particularly the powerful healing therapeutic force that is the doctor-patient relationship. This book will illustrate these changes as I observed them.

The book will also record the move from state hospital psychiatric care to community health centers through the story of Haverford State Hospital, a model psychiatric hospital built in suburban Philadelphia in 1962. At the time of its inception, it presented an entirely new model for housing and treating hospitalized mental patients.

Bella's story is about hope, overcoming the stigma of mental illness and the role that determination can play in life success. She was a role model of strength, endurance and caring for her children and husband, whom I also saw for therapy. Her accomplishments reinforce my firm belief that although psychiatric medications can facilitate improvement in mental disorders, it is people working with people, on a sustained long-term basis, that is equally or even more important, in maintaining recovery and producing emotional growth.

This is particularly relevant today when insurance restrictions often make it difficult to obtain complete and consistent psychiatric treatment.

Except for Bella and her immediate family, Bob, David and Becky, I have changed all first and last names, including Bella's maiden and married names. The only other exceptions are Drs. Dunn, Harris and Varner mentioned in the history of Osteopathic Psychiatry and Jack Kremens, M.D., the first superintendent at Haverford State Hospital.

Many people made it possible for me to write this book. First, I would like to thank Bella for sharing her life story with me and then giving me written permission to use my notes from her therapy sessions and write this book. Thanks also to her husband Bob and their two children, David and Becky, for their trust, their respect and for allowing me to use their therapy notes. Bob has been most helpful. I interviewed him several times. These interviews gave me insights into his life with Bella, their marriage, their parenting and their reactions to events at which I was not present. He has always been available to answer my questions. I have incorporated some of his beautiful and often insightful words. The written information that I had on all four of them in our therapy sessions as well as Bob's recollections allowed me to describe interactions and even re-create dialogue to the best of my ability, at times, when I was clearly not present.

My sincere thanks go to my teacher, mentor and friend Cecil Harris, D.O., FACN, for the background information on the history of Osteopathic Psychiatry and the Philadelphia Mental Health Clinic. Thank you to my wife, Alice, an extraordinary woman, for reading the final draft of this book, for her ongoing suggestions and support and for tolerating the intense concentration and focus often involved in writing. Kudos goes to my son, Fred, for reading and commenting on the first draft of this work and my daughter, Michelle for reading and commenting on parts of the text.

Thank you to my friend Jeffrey Kolansky, Esquire for researching the mental health acts mentioned in the text.

Much gratitude goes to journalist, author and memoir teacher, Anndee Hochman, for professionally editing my third draft. Her excellent margin notes and other suggestions were very helpful in allowing me to understand the various nuances that contribute to writing a memoir. She once commented, "Many memoir-writers have said that they didn't discover what they truly thought about something, or what an experience meant until they write it down." How true this is. Writing this book allowed me to sort out Bella's life but also various aspects of my own.

That will bring me to my parents to whom I have dedicated this book. Although I have shared with you some of negatives in our relationship, please remember that there was also much positive. As I grow older, I become even more aware of their true legacy to me. They raised me in a conservative Jewish home. The values and traditions that I learned there have sustained me and added to my life. My father's professional manner, ethics and caring ability with people is truly a gift. My mother's sense of style and generosity lingers with me always. Thank you both. I love you.

H Michael Zal
Lansdale, Pennsylvania

CHAPTER 1:
BELLA – A DANCE WITH MEDUSA

I met Bella for the first time six weeks into my three-year psychiatric fellowship. That day, I came to work at 8:30 AM, walked into the immense formal lobby of Haverford State Hospital's building four and took one of the elevators to the third floor. As the elevator doors opened, I heard a woman yelling, "Stop. Stop," in a high-pitched voice. There, down the hall near the women's ward, I saw an agitated young lady in a yellow and white dress. Her blond hair streamed down her back and flew from side to side as she screamed. She reminded me of Medusa, one of the Gorgon monsters of Greek mythology with snakes for hair. "Can't you see I'm the queen? How can you treat me this way?" She flailed her hands in a threatening manner, thought that she was royalty and yet seemed fearful that someone (Perseus and his forces?) was out to destroy her. The female psychiatric aide that had brought her from the first floor admissions suite, stood by frozen, looking frightened and helpless, not knowing what to do. The ring of metal keys in the aide's hand made a soft musical clanging sound as she trembled.

Scared and hesitant, I walked slowly down the hall concerned that if I looked at her, her deadly powers would turn me instantly into stone, as predicted in the Greek myth. When I reached where she was, I took her hand. She stopped screaming and looked at me with luminous blue eyes that emanated a translucent glow. I walked her gently toward the women's ward, three north, as you would lead someone onto a crowded dance floor, unlocked the door and took her to the nurse's station. She turned back, looked at me and smiled as the aide took her to her room.

The year was 1967. It was August. Actress Vivien Leigh, Scarlet O'Hara in Gone With the Wind, had just died at age 53 of tuberculosis; Stokely Carmichael called for a black revolution in the United States as race riots swept across our land and LBJ announced plans to send 45,000 more troops to Vietnam. My focus was elsewhere. I had just begun my psychiatric fellowship. Prior to this, I had completed a one-year rotating internship in Columbus, Ohio. This training had involved the medical management of patients under the supervision of an attending physician on various specialty services. I had no formal psychiatric experience except for a few medical school courses, a psychiatric rotation in my fourth year of medical school and a summer of employment in the Industrial Therapy Department at a state psychiatric hospital.

I felt overwhelmed during my first few months at Haverford State Hospital. My job involved a lot of responsibility. I asked many questions and learned by doing. As a ward or staff physician, I was put in charge of the psychiatric and medical management of 30-50 inpatients. This included the prescription of medication, individual and group therapy, as well as supervision of their milieu and activities. I also administered electroconvulsive therapy, saw 25-30 outpatients monthly and often did counseling of family members. Clerical work included dictation of progress notes, completion of insurance forms and letters to other agencies. I also worked in the admission suite on a rotating basis and presented periodic special case conference dissertations for staff education.

Bella was not my first patient. The hospital had already assigned fourteen other inpatients to my service during the prior month. I got my first patient after two weeks of orientation. Excited as could be and filled with fantasies of facilitating a magical cure, I rushed to the 3-N female unit to meet her. I opened the large metal door to enter the locked unit. Still a novice in this world, I had a strange feeling of happiness that I had the keys, which clearly defined me as staff and not a patient. I ran onto the unit to find Ms. Benita Benson lying on her back immobile and mute on the hallway floor. "I'm Dr. Zal," I said. She did not respond. She was catatonic. I lifted her arms and pulled her toward me. They remained where I left them. I attempted to move her. Her posture remained rigid. I watched in amazement as two male psychiatric aides carried her to her room. I stood there feeling helpless and inadequate. I almost wished that they had assigned me a patient with wild and unpredictable catatonic excitement rather than this stuporous, inactive and unresponsive catatonic schizophrenic woman on the floor.

The morning of my first interview with Bella, I unlocked the heavy door of 3-N women's unit eager but anxious to see the new patient who had been so regressed and disturbed two days earlier. Immediately the noise hit me. The female unit had a tone of uproar, commotion and confusion like the tower of Babel. I walked down the long, monotonous hallway to the small physician's office on the left. I passed the stark conference room, with its long wooden table and chairs, where we held our weekly new case conference. In front of the physician's office was the glass enclosed and locked nursing station, which isolated two psychiatric aides and a nurse, from the din of the large day room, as they busily took off orders and wrote notes in patient's charts. Small single and double patient rooms in front and to the right outlined the dayroom. I unlocked the doctor's office and entered quickly, happy to escape the racket.

I sat in the drab, 8' x 10', physician's office for a while and tried to relax. The room had a sterile feel, with its green walls, gray metal desk, chair and bookcase and single window. A desk lamp, phone and a panic button were the only accessories. My security blanket was the nineteenth printing of the Diagnostic and Statistical Manual of Mental Disorders, first edition, published by the American Psychiatric Association in August of 1966. The room lacked any element of warmth. It did not even have a picture or a wall calendar to soften its cold look. I took a deep breath, opened the metal patient chart with its multicolored paper dividers and reviewed her records including her past psychiatric history.

Bella was Haverford State hospital patient # 4032. She was 20 years old. The thought came to me that, at age 26, I was not much older. She had two prior psychiatric hospitalizations. She had been hospitalized for the first time in May of 1966 at age 19 at Dufur Hospital, Ambler, Pa. After 10 days, she had been transferred to the psychiatric unit at Misericordia General Hospital, Philadelphia, Pa. There, she received 12 electro shock treatments .She remained there until July of 1966 when she was discharged home. She apparently stayed well until a short time before her admission to Haverford State Hospital on August 16, 1967.

After reviewing the chart, I called the nursing station. Lorraine, an aide, brought Bella into the room to see me. I stood up and walked toward them extending my hand. Lorraine said, "Bella this is Dr. Zal. He would like to ask you some questions." Her hair had been brushed straight. She was neatly dressed in a hospital gown and seemed much younger than her stated age. Gone was the ferocity that I had seen previously. Now medicated, she was passive, withdrawn and walked slowly, scanning the room suspiciously. I said hello, shook her hand and introduced myself as warmly as I could. "I would like to get to know you and see how I can be of help. Will you take a seat here?" In a quiet voice, she answered, "I'm Bella," as she took a seat in a chair on the side of the desk. "I'm glad to meet you Bella," I said as I returned to my seat. She sat up straight with her back tensing firmly against the back of the metal chair and her hands folded tightly in her lap. She looked prim and proper. Two mental images came to my mind. On the one hand, she could have been a habited nun. On the other hand, I could picture her as an efficient secretary coming to work in a shirtwaist dress popular at the time with matching gloves, shoes and handbag. She was calmer but guarded, internally focused and still clearly psychotic. My job that day was to complete a standard mental status evaluation. I started by saying, "Bella, since it is our first meeting I will have to ask you many questions so I can get to know you and try to help. There are no trick questions. Just answer the best that you can."

I asked, "Bella can you tell me what date it is and where you are?" She knew it was Thursday, August 18, 1967 and that she was at Haverford State Hospital. "I thought that you would know that one," I quipped in an effort to relax her.

"Why are you here?"
"My mother was upset with me. I wouldn't do what she wanted."
I made a mental note to ask her about her relationship with her mother in future sessions.
"Bella, when you read a newspaper or watch television, can you focus and pay attention?"
"I can sometimes."
"How is your memory? Are you forgetful?"
"My memory is fine."

She was able to subtract serial sevens correctly (100-7 = 93; 93-7 = 86, etc.), but it took her a long time to complete the task. She seemed perplexed and distracted at times but I could see that she was trying to cooperate.

I asked her to read a selected paragraph from the hospital manual about the administration. She interpreted it in terms of her own delusional thoughts. "It means that I know that I have followers."

Bella's responses seemed flat, depressed and indifferent. When I asked her, "Do you feel depressed?" She answered, "a little." I asked her if she wished that she was dead or if she wanted to harm herself. She denied any thoughts of suicide and stated, "My conscience would tell me no. It would tell me to keep trying." I was glad to hear this and breathed a sign of relief.

Bella spoke in a slow manner and seemed anxious. She showed undirected restlessness during most of the interview. She impulsively picked up papers from the desk, walked around the room and even wrote her name in one of the books on my desk.

At one point, when she seemed to have withdrawn into herself, I asked her "Bella, what are you thinking about?"

"I feel very confused," she said. "People are trying to play tricks on me; the room is bugged. I can't talk freely inside a building."

Twice during the interview, the phone rang. Bella, who has been previously calm and withdrawn, became agitated and irritable. "I wish someone would answer that silly phone." The second time, I asked her, "Why did you get so upset when the phone rang?" She stated, "I feel this way because no one ever calls me."

Bella went on to tell me a long story, which jumped from one subject to another in a loose and round about manner. There were religious themes. Bella explained her current behavior as follows: "When I was little, I loved to daydream. The nuns at school told me stories about religious figures and their kind deeds. I would go home and hear the fighting and screaming and wanted things for myself and couldn't get them." She stated that she felt that she was different from other girls that had normal families. These answers gave me ideas for questions that I wanted to ask Bella in upcoming sessions.

When I asked her what she thought she might like to do in the future, she answered grandiosely, "I would like to help the country and President Johnson." She also stated, "I only want to get married and live a normal life. I need someone to take care of me."

She did seem vulnerable and helpless during this interview. As I got to know Bella better, I realized that when she was well, she radiated an innocence that was deceptive. In fact, she knew exactly what she wanted and how she wanted things to be done. This facade melted away when she was about to became psychotic. At these times, she faded like one of the tapered golden beeswax candles that she loved to make as an adult. What remained was a fragile, vulnerable, childlike inner core of molten wax that said, "Love me; protect me; save me."

"Bella have you ever heard a voice talking to you and you turned around and there really was no one there?" "No, she said, but sometimes, I heard crickets." "Have you ever seen visions?" I asked. She answered, "One time last year, while I was in the mountains, I saw something terrible, someone that was red, something that I did not understand that made me tremble"

"Bella, who are the last three presidents of the United Sates," I asked. She answered, "President Nixon, Kennedy and Johnson. I Liked Kennedy."

I asked, "What would it mean if someone said, 'People who live in glass houses shouldn't throw stones?" She answered, "People that think that they are so great can see bad within everyone else, but not within themselves. They are really the stones." In response to the proverb, 'Don't cry over spilt milk', she said, "Things I have done in the past should not be cried over."

Bella had some insight in that she realized that she was ill. She stated, "I hope that you can help me with my problems."

"We are finished for today. It was nice to meet you. Thank you for sharing your thoughts with me. I will see you again and I will try to help you with your problems. I'll take you back to the ward now." With that, I led her back into the day room. She walked slowly to the old spinet piano against the far wall and began to play Beethoven's Fur Elise, one of the few songs that I had learned by heart as a young piano student.

Latter that day, I wrote in her chart:

<u>Diagnostic Impression:</u>   Schizophrenia Reaction, Paranoid Type
000-x24

CHAPTER 2:
THE HAVERFORD HILTON

Six weeks earlier, I had crossed over Montgomery and Lancaster Avenues on the Philadelphia Main Line. I passed the back of the prestigious Haverford School and then the grounds of Haverford College. Soon I saw beautiful homes that lined both sides of College Avenue, with their manicured lawns, dense shrubbery, and circular driveways. I had not been here for two years and had forgotten the beauty of this road. However, I knew that in just a few minutes, I would come a long way from these magnificent palatial homes to a home for troubled souls. When College Avenue became a dead end, I made a right turn unto Darby Road.

There, I saw a five-foot high semicircular gray stone wall. I was surprised that there was no sign marking the transition from serene opulence to the psychiatric treatment facility that was Haverford State Hospital, at 3500 Darby Road, in Haverford, Pennsylvania. There was no gate or fence. I made a left turn. On one side of the narrow road,

I saw tall trees bordering a vacant lot. On the other side, flowering trees brought my eyes to a five story red brick building with two wings facing front. I saw a person looking out of one of the large, light blue-topped windows. This was building four, the admissions unit. My heart started beating faster with nervousness and excitement. The last time that I was here, I had been a student. This time, I was a physician.

I parked my steel blue triumph GT-6 in front of the building. I slid my thin six-foot frame out of the low-slung car. I became annoyed when I realized engine oil had dripped on my shoes. This was my first day at work and I wanted to present my self well. I smoothed down my kaki suit jacket, straightened my tan knit tie against my white starched shirt, and walked across the road. I entered building three, the administration building. I filled out some employment papers and received my keys. I also learned that as an Osteopathic Fellow in Psychiatry, through the Philadelphia Mental Health Clinic, under the auspices of the National Institute of Mental Health, the state would hire me as a Ward Physician with a class title of Staff Physician I. This position paid a salary of $14,612.00 a year. This was considerably more than I had ever made before. I had received $3,000 during my internship. This pay scale was more than double the salary that I would earn in the second and third year of my fellowship training at the outpatient clinic.

I literally danced down the road back to building four. I could not wait to tell my wife the good news. As a married twenty-six year old, with a one-year-old daughter, I felt truly rich. We spent $35.00 a week on food and incidentals. Our rent was $233.00 a month. For the first time in our married life, we would be ahead of the game. As I walked, I fantasized how we would splurge with my first paycheck. Perhaps we would have diner with friends at the Fireside Hearth or go to see

"On a Clear Day" at the Camden County Music Fair. Maybe, I could even buy my wife a belated birthday gift. When I reached building four, I stumbled on the curbstone and I looked up. It hit me that once I entered the door, that this building would become my world, where I would work, study, agonize and learn, for the next fifteen months.

On July 20, 1953, Pennsylvania Governor John S. Fine signed into law an act to allow construction of a mental hospital in Delaware County, Pennsylvania, in order to relieve overcrowding at Philadelphia State Hospital at Byberry and the state psychiatric hospitals in Norristown and Embreeville, Pennsylvania. The original time estimate was that it would take three years. Due to politics and neighborhood resistance, it took almost ten years. Haverford State Hospital did not open until October of 1962.

Aside from its location in a wealthy suburb of Philadelphia, Haverford State Hospital was unique in many other ways. Jack B. Kremens, M.D., its' first superintendent and my current boss felt that the hospital represented the "ideal" mental hospital because it provided treatment in the patient's own community. Although the hospital was relatively small, it offered a range of psychiatric services making it possible to meet the patients' individual needs. It was also distinctive because it placed important emphasis on research.

The most striking difference about this psychiatric hospital was the physical plant. To some, it was known as the "Haverford Hilton." I had also heard it referred to as the "Haverford County Club." Although you could only see building four from the main entrance road, the campus opened up to many surprises. Set on several acres of green grass and woodlands, it had a large recreation building, which included a gym, billiards and poolroom, a soda fountain, and a four-lane bowling alley. It had a library that could hold 4000 books. There was a central music room with five soundproof practice rooms and locker rooms for men and women volunteers. There was a 12, 400 square foot therapy building which housed both occupational and industrial therapy activities. Patients could learn crafts, woodworking, office procedures, homemaking, dressmaking, as well as do artwork. The industrial therapy program emphasized placing patients in jobs within the hospital, such as the canteen and ground crews.

Until this time, most inpatient psychiatric facilities made use of tall buildings where patients were housed in large wards. Haverford's building four, which housed new patients, was the hospital's only intensive care building and its only building with locked wards. Although this building resembled the older model psychiatric hospital in some ways, it was also unique. It had an admissions suite on the main floor with offices for psychiatrists to interview new patients, a psychological testing room, physical exam rooms and social service rooms. One wing housed a medical and surgical unit for 40 patients. There was X-ray equipment, an operating room, central supply and a high-speed sterilizer. The second floor housed a laboratory, a pharmacy, a dental lab and treatment room as well as rooms for physiotherapy, diathermy and whirlpool facilities. All of these features allowed doctors to do routine medical care on site.

The top three floors of building four each housed two locked wards, one for male patients and the other for female patients. Each closed ward with its own dining room and day room. There was a barbershop for the men and a beauty parlor for the women. The goal was to limit the patient's stay in the intensive care building to ninety days. Those patients who had not been discharged by this time and required longer care were transferred "down the hill" to smaller extended care buildings on the large campus. Here they would stay in a more family like therapeutic atmosphere until they were ready for discharge.

Once inside building four, I asked the volunteer at the front desk to page the third floor unit chief, an Osteopathic Psychiatrist named Dr. Paul Kaplan. He would be my main supervisor. While I waited, I thought about my last time in this building. I had been interested in psychiatry since college. To be sure, that my interest was practical and not just an intellectual pursuit, I took summer employment in 1965, while still a medical student, in the Industrial Therapy Department. I carried the professional responsibility of a therapeutic activity worker, which included patient counseling, assignment of patients to work areas and direct communication with staff psychiatrists. I was able to participate in all staff meetings and conferences including formal case presentations. My job also included being a work crew supervisor. I took 6-8 male patients out in an open field to cut down tall grass with a sickle. At the time, I thought nothing of it but years later, I wondered, what were they thinking sending psychiatric patients out into an open field with no fence with a sharp blade? Fortunately, there were no problems except that once I did cut my knee with the sickle and they had to take me to the Bryn Mawr Hospital emergency room for stitches. I enjoyed my work that summer. It helped me know that psychiatry was the right specialty for me.

I looked around at the grandeur of this edifice with its travertine marble walls and slate floor. Although I had been here before, I still felt intimidated. I wondered how patients felt when they walked from the admissions unit through this great hall. Before my mind could drift any further, Paul appeared. He was about five foot seven, stocky in build and wore a herringbone gray- green sport jacket, with a flowered

red and green tie and gray slacks. He seemed friendly and kind. He shook my hand firmly and said, "Welcome to Haverford State."

CHAPTER 3:
WARD THREE NORTH-FEMALE PATIENTS

As Bella played the piano, I stood and watched the circus like atmosphere of the day room. What a cast of characters. There were paranoid schizophrenics, who sat on the edge of their chairs or paced up and down the square room scanning the atmosphere for danger. Others, in mismatched clothing, talked to imaginary people. There was one small table with two chairs in the corner. Here sat a depressed and anxious middle-aged woman, from the Philadelphia Main Line, who was addicted to pain medications, with her hands tensely clenched, quite fearful of her ward mates. In the other chair sat an older patient, looking confused and picking nervously at her food stained hospital gown. An attractive patient, wearing high heels and a flowered red and white dress, banged on the nursing office door demanding attention. A 48-year-old woman, who had come in with a diagnosis of Psychoneurotic disorder, depressive reaction was beginning to show a more severe degree of diminished energy, walked slowly from one end of the room to the other. Against the wall, two catatonic patients sat quietly looking into space.

In the center ring stood Ms. Loretta Brown., a twenty two year old paranoid schizophrenic, who was mildly mentally deficient. She wore a brown skirt, with white socks and dirty white sneakers topped off with an oversized green hospital gown. As Bella played the piano, Loretta danced to the music, round and round in a circular motion. She squeezed a half of an orange onto her head. As the juice ran down her closely cropped African American hair and onto her face, she laughed and laughed. Loretta was a powerful force whose shenanigans and story would stay in my memory for the rest of my life. Many years later, after the above incident, Bella and I would both remember this moment. Several weeks later, during a similar incident, Bella made the mistake of laughing at Loretta's behavior. Loretta stopped squeezing oranges and hit Bella in the face breaking her nose. She had to be taken to the medical unit on the first floor of building four. Loretta was placed in an isolation room.

Soon after returning to the ward, Bella went to talk to Loretta. Standing outside the door of the small isolation room, Bella could see, through the small window that Loretta had removed all of her clothes and was lying naked on a mattress on the floor in a fetal position. "I'm sorry that I laughed at you. I really like you. May God bless you and make you well," Bella said. At first, Loretta said nothing. Then she responded in a baby voice, "Goo Goo Ga Ga," and spit at Bella. After that, in a very small quiet voice she offered the words, "I'm scared." Bella responded, "Don't worry, I get scared sometimes too." Loretta just looked at her and her eyes filled up with tears. From then on there was a new bond between them.

Loretta frustrated me. Later in my fellowship training, I would probably have tried to conceptualize her in the Freudian model as being all about sexual and aggressive drives. However, at this point I just saw Loretta as impossible. During our talks, she alternated between baby talk and coming on to me sexually. She voiced bizarre somatic delusions including, "My stomach smells. Why are my feet so big? Cut off my legs." She occasionally seemed to be responding to auditory hallucinations. I treated her with a combination of phenothiazines. She showed some improvement but remained physically and verbally abusive.

A week after breaking Bella's nose, she assaulted two patients and attacked an attendant who had come to bring her food in the seclusion room. I had to do something before Loretta hurt more people. We decided to give her electric convulsive treatments. (ECT) After 20 treatments, she showed remarkable improvement. She became sociable, helpful to others, and cooperative. She denied all knowledge of her prior antics. Gradually, she verbalized a desire to gain employment, care for her two illegitimate children and increase her self-sufficiency. In February, I transferred her to building 11 where her new psychiatrist subsequently released her on a trial visit.

Mary Renolyds, RN, the head nurse of unit 3N, dressed in her starched white uniform complete with a matching white nurse's cap, that represented her nursing school, was the one that kept order in all this chaos. She was a very special lady. Pragmatic, insightful and kind, she went about her job methodically. Nothing seemed to faze her. Her special greeting, "how are you dear?" somehow made you feel secure and cared for. She had two male aids and a female aid that helped her. They all treated her with respect and came to her with their problems. From day one, we had a good rapport. She was a mentor to me and helped me find my way in a new professional environment. She made me feel welcome, accepted and respected. Her eyes sparkled and she smiled warmly anytime that she saw me. She listened to me when I felt irritable and discouraged. She shared her professional experience and made helpful treatment suggestions without making me feel inadequate. We gradually became friends.

One day, Mary handed me an envelope stating, "Bella gave me this to mail. I thought you would want to see it" The envelope was addressed to "The President of the U.S.A. Washington D.C." The return address in the upper left hand corner of the envelope read: "Bella A. Devlin, Haverford State Hospital, Haverford, Pennsylvania 19064." Bella had attached a blue and white 5-cent U.S. George Washington postage stamp. Inside the envelope was a note on white paper with three red roses on the cover. It read: There will be many many wars, I do not care to travel to Europe – for I believe we should discover America first. I will remain faithful to <u>God</u> and to <u>my</u> country. I am <u>queen</u> and I <u>am</u> King. I know where I am going –

Initially, Bella was grandiose, paranoid, distrustful and preoccupied with religious themes. I started her on an antipsychotic medication called Stelazine (trifluoperazine), because I felt that it would help diminish her paranoid delusions and since it was less sedating than the other phenothiazine antipsychotics. I worried about the development of side effects. I added the antiparkinsonian drug Cogentin (benztropine) and watched her carefully for tremor, protrusion of the tongue, mask-like facies, a shuffling gait, and a host of other possible neuromuscular and extrapyramidal side effects. I watched for any complaints of sore throat, sores in her mouth and throat, pain upon swallowing or increased temperature. I ordered blood tests periodically to be sure she had not developed a low white blood count or toxic effects to her liver. The other residents kidded me about the "purple people" because of the purplish pigmentation of the skin that could occur in patients receiving high doses of Stelazine over a long period. As a psychiatrist, there was so much to be concerned about when you placed a patient on medication. Fortunately, no side effects occurred to Bella. On these carefully dosed medications and large doses of supportive psychotherapy, she gradually showed improvement.

She became more trustful and less grandiose and delusional. Her religiosity diminished. She participated more in the morning ward group meeting. She was given group privileges and attended horticultural therapy in the green house. She started to focus on helping others. She volunteered to help the aids make beds. She called patients to come to the nursing station to get their medications. She tried to relax the patients who paced the halls. She watched another patient crochet and tried to learn. However, Loretta was her favorite. Bella loved playing the piano for her and enjoyed seeing her dance.

I often wondered why these two opposite personalities had become friends. I suspect that somehow Bella envied Loretta's carefree behavior that was in direct contrast to her own more rigid and perfectionist ways. Loretta also dealt with her anger a lot more directly. I discovered another clue when I met Loretta's mother. Mrs. Brown, attractive and well dressed, presented herself aristocratically. She was thin and was always dressed in pastel sweater sets with matching purse and high heels popular at the time. Her nails and makeup were perfect. She tried endlessly to get Loretta to conform to this image. Loretta, unable to do this, rebelled mocking her mother's rigid behavior and girly ways. Her clown makeup and her naked dancing spoke of her sexuality but made fun of everything that her mother stood for. Before her admission, Loretta had gone on a crash starvation diet and lost fifty pounds. Subsequently, she ran into a neighbor's house yelling, "My mother is trying to kill me." The way I see it, both Bella and Loretta had ambivalent feelings toward their mothers. Their friendship offered them each a modicum of maternal-like acceptance, admiration and love. On some level, they understood each other and connected emotionally.

As she got better, Bella became more assertive. One day, she got dressed in her yellow and white cotton dress and white pumps. Instead of waiting for the group to go out on the grounds, Bella waited at the ward door until a student nurse unlocked it. She then walked out and took the tunnel between building four and the recreation building that was used to transport patients if the weather was bad. Once there, she walked next door and went into the personnel office in Building three and applied for a job as a secretary. It took them a while to figure it out and to realize that she was a patient. The staff was very upset when they found out what she had done. This assertive behavior reminded me of another time in October of 1967, the month before Bella's transfer, when I had received an office memo from Kathie Darnel, RN, the nursing supervisor.

"Dr. Zal – Bella sent this note to Mr. Oland on 10-4-67. I spoke to her about it and she said she had read about Dr. George's staff meeting on a bulletin board and decided she wanted to attend! She typed this note in Mr. Oland's office before he found her and sent her back to the clerical pool." The note read as follows:

SUBJECT: Conference Room
TO: Dr. George – Dr. Zal
FROM: Isabelle A. Devlin
Dr. George:
If there is going to be a meeting in building three today of all
the staff members would I be able to attend (in the back of the
room)?
I will be in this building until 11:00 a.m. contact Mrs. Darnel.
Many thanks
      Isabelle Devlin

I showed Bella the memo and asked as kindly as I could, "What's this all about?" She answered with a sly smile, "I thought they could use some help." Somewhat exasperated but amused, I countered with, "Bella, Bella, what are we going to do with you?" She smiled coyly and walked away.

As the weeks went by, my other patients also started to improve. However, even as the older patients got better, the din in the Three North day room continued as new patients were admitted. There were anxious patients nervously wringing their hands along with the occasional confused older person in a Geri chair sitting on the periphery watching the center of the room with dull eyes who grabbed at you at you walked by. Excited catatonic schizophrenics showed wild ceaseless movement. Paranoid schizophrenics responded to their inner voices. Manic women, fueled by over productive energy, waltzed by seductively, dressed in bright colored clothing with matching heavy necklaces and bracelets, and added color to an otherwise monotonous gray-green environment. At times, they would make inappropriate sexual advances to the male aids and doctors. This behavior was quite embarrassing, the first time it happened to me. Estrogen filled the room.

The manic patients were not the only ones who had sex on their minds. One day Loretta came up to me and said, "Dr. Zal I want to have sex with you." Busy and overwhelmed with work as usual, I chidingly told her, "You'll have to make an appointment." Loretta and her antics, alternating between assaultive hostile behavior and simple-minded clowning around, continued to cause everyone to feel fearful and yet at times smile at the extreme apparent senselessness of it all. At times, she would remove her clothes in the dayroom, apply her make-up in a bizarre clown mask-like fashion and continued to rub oranges into her hair.

Looking back, I realized that the blatant verbal and physical sexuality and the open hostility sometimes show by some of the regressed male and female patients on the closed wards must have been quite shocking and foreign to me. At the time, I handled the stress by relying on my façade of professional calm that my father had taught me and tightening up inside. My parents send me messages about sex and anger that made it clear to me that they were not comfortable with either. My Father tried to tell me the facts of life by reading from Genesis. "And Cain knew his wife; and she conceived…and Irad begot Mehujael; and Mehujael begot Methushael; and Methushael begot Lamech." At the time, I thought that it was hilarious and walked out of the room. My mother slapped my hand when, at age seven, sitting next to her on the couch, I touched her clothed breast out of curiosity. They never spoke of anything even remotely sexual. My father either did not acknowledge anger or showed it through irritability toward his children. My Mother showed it only indirectly by tears or her constant complaining. Sometimes, I feel that I wasted my youth on this tense and inhibited young man who coped with anxiety provoking situations by closing up to maintain control rather than embracing the moment. My journey toward comfort with sex and aggression began at Haverford State.

The average length of stay on a locked unit, for my patients, at this time was approximately two months. At this juncture, some of the patients, who had shown enough improvement and could handle a more open setting, were transferred to a small extended treatment building with a cottage like setting down the hill on the sprawling hospital grounds. Here they would receive additional treatment under professional supervision but could move around the grounds on their own, eat in the cafeteria in building 21 and attend recreational activities in building 20 until they were thought to be ready for discharge. Often their doctor allowed them one or two home or trial visits prior to discharge to test their behavior.

After almost three months on a closed unit, the staff felt that Bella was doing better but was still fragile emotionally. At disposition conference, it was decided that she should remain in the hospital, because of the severity of her regression upon admission and her prior history of psychiatric hospitalization, but that she no longer required the protection of a locked unit. They say that it takes three months to get used to a new job and go through the learning curve. Just as I was getting to feel comfortable in my new position, I transferred Bella to open Building 12, under the care of Dr. Bruce Hammond, a kindly middle-aged psychiatrist. In this extended treatment building, she would continue her medication, attend group and individual psychotherapy and test her wings to see how she could handle additional freedom outside of the confines of a locked unit.

CHAPTER 4:
THE OSMOND BUILDINGS

On November 06, 1967, the United States changed its campaign plan by becoming more offensive in the Vietnam War. On that day, they bombed the biggest supply depot in North Vietnam. Compared to the world at large, life at Haverford State Hospital was calm and peaceful. That was the day that the hospital changed Bella's treatment plan in an effort to encourage her to be more independent and move her closer to discharge. After 83 days confined to a locked ward in building four, she was transferred to an extended care building on the grounds of the hospital. This decision met the 90-day goal for an intensive care stay.

That morning, Bella had breakfast and attended the ward meeting where she said goodbye to Nurse Mary, the psychiatric aides and the other patients. She had already told Loretta the night before that she was being moved down the hill. After the meeting, an aide, Lillie, escorted her through the locked heavy door of ward three north, down the elevator, across the lobby and out the double doors of building four. The sky was clear and bright. She was wearing the same yellow and white dress that she had on the day that she was admitted to the hospital. I suspect, a little distrustful of change, she held her bag of possessions close to her chest and admitted, "I'm scared." Lillie probably reassured her, "Don't worry. You will be fine. You'll like Building 12." Across the road, Bella could see building three, the administration building. It housed the employment office where, earlier in her hospital stay, she had snuck off the ward to seek a job.

Bella and Lillie turned right and walked down the road past the recreation building. Here the path split to reveal several smaller buildings on each side of a grassy knoll. On the right side was the occupational therapy building and extended care buildings 14 and 15. On the left side were extended care buildings 10, 11, 12, 13 and 17. In the distance, at the end of the grass area was a perpendicular road along which stood two large one story geriatric buildings for the treatment of older patients. If you turned right from the end of either of the arms of the "Y" and continued around the curve, you would reach building 20, a dining facility, where all extended care patients ate their meals.

They turned onto the left fork and approached extended care building 12. Bella must have been pleased at what she saw. In contrast to the noisy, often threatening, drab atmosphere of the closed ward in Building four, this building, built of brick and aluminum on the outside and tile on the inside, was inviting and pleasant. She walked through the front doorway to find a bright, cheerful lobby with hallways to the left and right. As she waited for Lillie to check her in at the reception desk, she would note that each side of the building was a mirror image containing a physician's office, an examination room, a visitor's room and an Occupational Therapy room. At the end of each were a nursing station and a ward kitchen. The staff used this kitchen to store evening snacks or to provide meals for patients who were home bound due to minor physical illness. At the far end of each hall was a large well-lit day room.

The receptionist would ask Bella and Lillie to turn left and check in at the nursing station at the end of the hall. As she waited for the nurse to welcome her, I imagine that Bella observed the inviting day room with its comfortable furniture, ping-pong table, television and a good supply of games, crafts, books and magazines. She would see male and female patients playing monopoly or reading the newspaper. Through the windows of the day room was a flagstone patio with tables and chairs where patients sat talking and enjoying the sunshine.

Probably a little fearful and yet excited, Bella said goodbye to Lillie and followed the nurse, Jessica Walters, RN, a stern looking tall woman, through the 46 by 54 foot day room. Jessica most likely told her" You will share this day room with twenty-four patients, men and women. There are certain rules you will have to follow. I will give you a list." I imagine Bella must have been startled for a moment by Nurse Jessica's gruff manner and at the thought that the day room was coed. She probably did not say a word but just kept walking. From here, she was led through a small four-patient sitting room, which was painted robin's eggshell blue. Looking around, she could see the bathroom, containing two shower stalls, two toilets, two sinks and a bathtub. There were doors at either end of the bathroom so that her three pod mates as well as the four female patients in the adjoining pod could share it. These eight people would constitute a therapy group. There were two pods on the other side of the day room, which housed eight male patients. Two additional pods occupied the sidewall of the day room. Lastly, she was shown into one of the four single bedrooms that had her name on the door. Bright, clean, and painted off white, it contained a single bed with attractive yellow and blue bed linens, a bookshelf, small desk and chair, and a window with bright yellow curtains. This would be her room for some time.

Bella's new home, Building 12, was one of five "Osmond type" buildings on the hospital grounds. The hospital modeled its extended care buildings after the theories of British psychiatrist, Humphry Fortescue Osmond, M.D. Prior to attending medical school, he worked for an architect in Surrey, England. When he immigrated to Canada, to head up the large custodial mental institution in Weyburn, Saskatchewan, his two interests, architecture and psychiatry merged in a way that would forever change psychiatric inpatient care. In Weyburn, he saw the inhumane warehousing of patients in large wards that represented institutionalized care at the time. He joined with Canadian architect, Kyoshi "Joe" Izumi to evaluate the effect that hospital design had on the progression of psychosis and on interpersonal relationships. They created a treatment environment that would encourage growth rather than isolation and dependency.

He suggested three levels of social relationship that could have architectural counterparts that would be beneficial to good patient care. He proposed a pie shaped configuration that would allow patients to be alone in a personal space when they needed to retreat. When ready for interpersonal relationships, they could move into a space with a limited number of people and then progress into a larger space where they could relate to even more people. Patients could move freely between these three spaces. Haverford State Hospital's "Osmond like buildings," did not copy Dr. Osmond's circular building with its pie wedge design. However, they did provide his "three level" concept in the form of a double "Y-shaped" structure where each side of the building had six units, each consisting of 4 private rooms, which lead into a small sitting room and a shared bathroom. From here, the patients, like Bella, could move into the larger common space of the day room when they were ready for additional social interaction.

Bella's transfer to the protective but open nest of building 12, under the care of Drs. Bruce and Anna Hammond, not only helped her prepare for life outside the hospital but also produced a life long friendship with this nurturing couple. Dr. Bruce was at Haverford State Hospital from the beginning. He was tall and thin, wore horned rimed glasses and smiled easily. His wife, Dr. Anna, after staying at home to raise their three children joined Dr. Bruce, as a part time psychiatrist in Building # 12 in 1965. She was also thin and tall and had short gray hair. Her gentle caring manner fitted in well with the atmosphere of the building. She worked three days a week. Dr. Bruce took care of her patient's on the days she was not there.

Each "Osmond-like building" had its own flavor. Building 12 was a mix of "crazies" as the staff affectionately called them. However, it was a place that the patients liked to go. The building was a happy place where the patients and staff members treated each other with respect. The staff could talk and "bitch" to each other. The staff's approach was part therapy, part parental and part friend. Jessica Walters, R.N., the head nurse on the unit, known by colleagues and patients as being firm, brusque and tough as a staff sergeant, demanded that you follow the rules and regulations. However, she also had a reputation as being kind and the patients' loved her. At a time when staff still treated many hospitalized psychiatric patients as dependent children, this was a welcome change. Dr. Anna must have been well aware of this having worked at the older Philadelphia State Hospital where this often occurred.

Her approach was gentler but both she and Nurse Jessica agreed in what would later be called "tough love." In building 12, Dr. Anna ran a therapy group one day a week. The hospital community knew that she told her patient's, "You don't have to come to group. However, if you do attend, there are certain ground rules. You have to behave yourself. I know it will be hard for some of you. I expect you to act as a grownup in and out of the group. I will treat you with respect and I expect the same from you." One day after special care conference in building four, she shared with me, "You have a sick patient who is a human being and is no more responsible for his or her craziness than they would be if they had a gastric ulcer. You treat the symptoms of their illness and treat them as a human being rather than just giving them another does of medication and putting them in restraints. If they see a little kindness, they will pick up on it to."

At first Bella was lonely in Building 12. She missed the hustle and bustle of three north. She missed Loretta's excitement and playing the piano. She missed Nurse Mary's pleasant manner. Gradually, she adjusted. She liked talking to the Drs. Hammond. She attended group therapy and sat quietly as others told their sad stories, absorbing and feeling their pain. She was given ground privileges and worked in the clerical pool. She drew pictures in art therapy and learned to knit in the occupational therapy building. She watched patients bowling in the recreation building and eating snacks in the canteen. At first, she wandered the grounds by herself and made the long walk to building 20 alone to eat her meals.

As she felt more comfortable, she returned to form. She started once again to help others and play a more active role in the building. She put away the magazines and books in the dayroom. She helped serve the snacks. She became friendly with a young woman named Madrilène. Bella liked her spontaneous carefree style. They would walk to building 20 together and sit at the same table to eat. They watched the male patients playing hoops and cheered for building 12 during the intramural baseball games. They went to the gym in the recreation building, sat around, and talked over cokes in the hospital canteen. They returned each afternoon to the building for the required one-hour rest time.

While Bella was down the hill, life went on in the world. War was the main theme. Secretary of State Dean Rusk said there was no turning back from Vietnam and anti-war protesters collided with police in New York City. Joan Baez mixed politics with song and protested against the war. There were also many distractions. People were reading Chaim Potock's The Chosen and William Styron's The Confessions of Nat Turner. The Beatles' were singing "All You Need Is Love." The Rolling Stones were entertaining us with "Ruby Tuesday." Moviegoers enjoyed Antonioni's "Blow Up," and Arthur Penn's "Bonnie and Clyde." NASA sent the Apollo 4 capsule into orbit from Cape Kennedy and launched a successful test of Saturn V. David Eisenhower announced his engagement to Julie Nixon.

The microwave oven appeared in stores for the first time. Navy beat Army 19-14 in football in Philadelphia.

My professional and personal life also went forward. My wife, I and our year- and- a- half- year old daughter were enjoying our first apartment in Philadelphia as a family. We lived at the Watergate apartments overlooking Fairmount Park. It was a four story building in an area of other apartment houses and small row homes. Although, we were on the second floor, our apartment opened onto a private patio and a larger shared grassed-in central courtyard. Much like the "Osmond like buildings," we could go from the privacy of our bedroom into the larger living room space and out the patio door to socialize with neighbors, many of whom were young couples our age with small children.

We enjoyed going to Barson's Deli in Wynnefield for ice cream so that we could watch our daughter smear ice cream all over her mouth and chin. On weekends, we often went to the Philadelphia Zoo. Our daughter dressed in her aqua snowsuit with her "big girl dress" sticking out of the bottom rode in her stroller looking happily at the animals and holding a red balloon. We drove to New York to visit my in-laws. The tolls were $2.50. On special nights, we would get a babysitter for $4.00 and perhaps go to dinner at our favorite Italian restaurant, Freddie's in downtown Philadelphia or Gatsby's restaurant on Montgomery Avenue in Merion. Sometimes, we would go to the movies. That winter, we saw Dustin Huffman and Anne Bancroft in "The Graduate", directed by Mike Nichols.

During this time, I cared for seventy-four inpatients and twenty-seven outpatients. I dealt with patients who were personality disorders, sociopaths and sexual deviates and those with psychoneurotic disorders such as depression and anxiety and situational reactions. I saw alcoholics and drug addicts and patients with organic brain syndromes as well as involutional psychotic reactions. I took histories, listened to patients, and tried my best to share perspective and hope. I learned to dose drugs such as Thorazine, Mellaril, Trilafon, Librium and Valium. I began to feel more like a psychiatrist.

Patients in both the intensive and extended care buildings were allowed to have visitors in the afternoon and evening. The hospital encouraged family meetings with or without the patient present and stressed the importance of family involvement in the patient's treatment plan. Between starting at Haverford and Bella's transfer to building 12, I had taken care of 29 inpatients and had interviewed 42 in-patient relatives. I do not remember Bella's family ever coming to visit.

After several day and weekend visits, Bella was sent home to her family on a trial visit on 12-19-67. This meant that she could return to the hospital at any time without having to sign new commitment papers or return to court. This made it easier for parents or relatives. Some patients' did well in the structure of the hospital but went home and soon fell apart emotionally. Bella seemed happy to be returning home. Amid all this contentment, a storm was brewing in both of our lives.

CHAPTER 5:
A PARENT'S LOVE

People do not grow up until they resolve their relationship with their parents. A woman especially must come to terms with her issues with her mother and a man must work out his relationship with his father. Bella and I stayed on this train to maturity for a long time. It took me some time to balance my negative and positive feelings about my father. Bella did not resolve her issues with her mother until almost the end of her life.

One day in therapy, I asked Bella, "Bella tell me about your parents?"

"My family gives the word dysfunctional a whole new meaning," she said. "They resent it when things are going well for you. They gloat when things are going badly for you. My mother and father center on themselves. The children come last. When I was in high school, I had to have my wisdom teeth taken out and had to stay overnight at a hospital. They dropped me off at the hospital and went on vacation."

"They sound very self centered," I said, "How did this make you feel?"

"I felt very neglected and unloved. As a child, I thought that they hated me."

At other times in therapy, when Bella talked about her family, there were certain themes that came up often. She related that her parents physically and mentally abused her. She felt angry that they said that everything was her fault. She harbored much guilt about her negative thoughts toward her mother. However, on the other hand, she said that they all came to her for support, particularly her mother and older sister. This behavior confused her. "They hate me and yet they want me to do everything."

In another session, Bella related, "I was physically afraid of my parents. My mother would spank me with a belt until I wet myself. When I was in 9th grade, she grabbed my hair and smashed my head through a glass window because I woke her up when she was taking a nap. She then locked me in my room because she was afraid that I would get blood on the floor. See, I have a scar over my left eyebrow. I have terrible guilt feelings about my mother. She always says that she puts her very best out for me. However, my sisters and I see the other side. She could drink until she became unconscious. She harassed the neighbors. She stole things from people's homes. Sometimes, I really feel that she is Satan."

"That must have been frightening to you. You have a right to feel angry about your mother's behavior. Physical abuse is unacceptable. What was your father like?"

My father was an alcoholic. Sometimes, he would sit in a dark room, smoking cigarettes and listening to classical music. He drank and picked on me. He was always angry and had an explosive temper. I would not make eye contact with him at the dinner table because I never knew how he would react. He broke my brother Will's leg when he as seven and I was nine. I was scared of him.'

"I don't blame you for feeling scared. That sounds terrifying, Bella. How did you cope with all that?"

Her tone softened and her eyes glazed over, as she responded, "I used to go and visit my grandmother a lot. She loved me." Her grandmother supplied the only love and acceptance that Bella had experienced up until that point. Her grandmother also took responsibility for raising Bella's older sister, Rose Marie. Their visits to their grandmothers' provided the only calm and stability that they had in their early years. In therapy one day, Bella lovingly shared the sense of contentment and security that she felt there: "My Grandmother lit candles and put them on the dining room table to set the mood for dinner whenever we ate there. We always ate together." Bella would continue this custom in her own house. Her memory of her grandmother's candles also fostered her interest, later in life, in making candles and other decorative objects out of bee's wax.

Bella's story stirred something inside of me. I could identify with her relationship with her grandmother. When she mentioned her, I smiled knowingly to myself. I could understand the value of having such a person in your early life. My maternal grandmother had also given me the gift of unconditional love. She was not physically affectionate, but her quiet presence in our home added a sense of security and caring to my world. I called her Bubba Paul. I was her first grandchild. Whenever I walked into the room and saw her face brighten, I felt special. Although she had her own home and did not live with us on a regular basis, she visited often. She was a quiet, unassuming, moody woman. A car hit my grandfather, crossing the Roosevelt Boulevard to attend synagogue, one Saturday morning, when I was age four and one-half. She would often get depressed living alone in her home. She would call my Mother, who would send my Father to go get her, and she would stay with us for a few days or a few weeks. She loved to bake and help with the housework. I remember her in the kitchen making her special cookies, which she called "Ss and Os because of their shape." Otherwise, she sat, quiet and content, next to a window watching people, traffic, or just nature.

She passed away at age 82 during my junior year of medical school. I can still see her now, a heavy set woman, wearing a cotton shirtwaist dress with a thin belt of matching material, black oxford shoes and on special occasions a single strand of pearls, with her thin, salt and pepper hair pulled straight back in a small bun. Whenever I saw her, her eyes lit up and her slight smile clearly communicated, "I love you. You are special." Her name was Machle. In English, people called her Molly. We named our first child, a daughter, Michelle in her honor.

Another time, I asked, "Bella, what else do you remember about how your parents treated you?"

"When I was with my parents, they made me feel horrible. They picked on me a lot because I was skinny. My mother often said: "Bella could be so pretty if she didn't have an ear that stuck out." My father teased me. He said- 'if I filled you with tomato juice, we could use you as a thermometer." Bella took these comments to heart and they damaged her self-esteem for the rest of her life. We would spend much time in therapy trying to get her to see herself as the attractive worthwhile woman that she was.

"Bella, do other people give you positive feedback about your looks?" She though for a while and then hesitantly answered, "Yes." "Perhaps you need to believe them."

"Bella, did you have any brothers or sisters," I asked. "Did talking to them about your experiences help you?"

"I have two brothers and three sisters. I am the second eldest. My sister, Rosemarie, is 12 months older than I am. She was a wacko. She was also hospitalized here. I was always made to feel guilty for her problems. I was always forced to take care of her. Even at age eleven, she had behavioral problems. I was attending public school and she was in Catholic School. My mother made me switch to Archbishop Prendergast High School (a catholic girls school in Upper Darby, Pa.) so I could keep an eye on her. Will was two years younger than I was. He was my favorite. Mary Kay was six years younger. She never had a breakdown but has a bad temper like my father. Ann is eight years younger than I am. She has had many breakdowns and often needed hospitalization. Luke is the baby. I often take care of him. There was no one except for my grandmother that I could talk to."

My family was not like Bella's family. However, my own emotional baggage resonated with some of her emotional pain. I could relate to her difficulties coming to terms with her Mother. In my case, it was my relationship with my Father that colored much of my life. My father was a quiet man, who was raised in a strict Jewish orthodox family. From what I remember of him, my grandfather appeared serious, aloof in his dark suit and high-hat, when on occasion, he came to our house for Friday night Shabbat dinner. He died when I was seven. My grandmother was an attractive woman with thick gray hair, more outgoing and was very active in Jewish charities. She was intense and decisive. She was more pleasant often offering to make me her hamburgers filled with onions and carrots. I can still remember the click clack of her high heals as she walked quickly down the street to synagogue. My father came to the United States from Latvia at age eleven with his two sisters. He grew up to become a man who took care of others and treated them with patience and kindness. All of his life, he saw himself as the caregiver of his family. They called on him to solve all problems. He became an attorney with a family type general practice. His clients also were very dependent on him.

He married a woman, seven years younger than himself, who also relied on his apparent strength and reliability but who complained about him all of their married life. My mother often used me to ventilate her angst. Affection was not her best suit. She over protected me. She said that she often did not sleep nights worrying about me. She kept me clean and well fed. She would listen to me if I were upset. When I was in the hospital for medical problems, she would walk twenty blocks to see me. She could be generous financially and never came to our house without bringing us something. As an adult, I realized that these acts were her way of showing love. Unfortunately, the word love was not in her vocabulary and never crossed her lips. Nor were there any touching, hugs and kisses or physical expressions of affection. My mother felt neglected because of my father's attention to his family and the community. The way that I see it, she wanted nurturing which he could not give her. He handled her demands for attention by withdrawing into a world of work and philanthropic activities. These were two things that he could do well and that made him feel good. My father's absence and my mother's inability to show warmth or affection left me feeling isolated and alone as a child. I could relate to this aspect in Bella.

I could also relate to the abuse that Bella suffered as a child. In spite of his gift with others, my father had no patience with me. When I was in elementary school, he punished me for minor infractions (I was a good kid) by hitting me with a strap. After he hit me, he made me stand in the corner with my hands straight down at my side. He told me not to move until he said so. I remember staring straight ahead with tears streaming down my face for long periods. At the time, my only response was crying. It was not until years later that I realized how humiliated, inadequate and angry I had felt at these times. My mother must have been around somewhere. I always wondered why I never heard them discuss my behavior or punishments. All that I remember is my father and I and the corner. During the few times that he would endeavor to help me with my homework, he quickly became intolerant and dismissed me. My father never complimented me. It was not until after he died that

I learned from others how proud he had been of my interests and accomplishments.

My childhood home had a large front room, painted white that served as both my father's law office and our family den. In this room, I had a small desk that faced the sidewall. Across the way, separated by two large front windows, facing the other wall, my father also had a desk. His was larger and made of dark mahogany. Often, we sat back to back doing work. We never spoke. We just did our work. The only thing that broke the silence was the occasional clanking sound of the trolley that passed in front of the house. In one back corner of this room between the wall and a large window with white venetian blinds, was the crying corner, where I stood after he hit me. The other back corner contained a couch with red and tan flowered slipcovers and two large rectangular foam rubber pillows.

One of my fondest memories was sitting on the couch in this room near my father watching the Gillette Friday Night Fights on the small television that stood next to the three shelved glass and dark wood bookcase that held his law books and the Hebrew books that his father had brought over from Russia. I longed to be closer to him but there was always a wall of tension between us. Looking back, in this sterile physical and emotional environment, I felt alone and unloved. I can now see another reason why Bella's case caught my attention. My childhood angst was minimal compared to the factors that shaped Bella's life. However, I could identify with her wanting love, approval and acceptance. On some level, I could understand her ambivalence toward her mother and her desire to cross the barrier of anger and tension that separated them. I felt that same way about my father.

It took more than ten years after he died for me to put my father in perspective, let go of some of my anger and realize how much I loved him. Around age 40, I was able to take my father off his pedestal of perfection and see him as a human being who had flaws and insecurities. As I grew older, had more life experiences, and children of my own, I began to understand my father better and realized that he loved me and that he did the best that he could. I often wondered how long it would take Bella to reach this stage. Now as I say the mourner's Kaddish in synagogue on the "Yahrzeit" (anniversary) of his death, on the Hebrew calendar, I strongly feel my sense of loss but I am thankful having been blessed with such a special father. I talk to him as I light a twenty-hour memorial candle at home at sunset and tell him what has happened to my family and me during the year. I ask him to watch over and help those who need his attention. I also tell him that I love him and that I am sorry that we were never able to connect in the way that I now know we both wanted.

The lit candle, the Rabbi tells me, is a fulfillment of the Psalmist's claim that "the soul of a person is a light for God". My second book, The Sandwich Generation: Caught Between Growing Children and Aging Parents was dedicated "In memory of Frank Zal, Esquire (1910-1968) whose light continues to shine on me."

Although Bella and I lived in two parallel worlds, had different genetics and followed very different paths, I could identify with her feelings of frustration and pain. No, I could not identify with her delusions when she was psychotic. It took psychiatric medications to mediate these biological symptoms. However, when she reconstituted, I spent time in therapy trying to give her a perspective and help her heal the hurt child within her. I tried to grow up with her again and understand her traumas as well as her hopes and dreams. I used my empathy to try to talk to the unique adult that she was and at times served as a cheerleader for her positive aspects. The process that we started in 1967 would continue off and on for many years. It took her many decades to resolve her feelings of love and anger toward her parents, particularly her mother. During these years, I was also in the process of resolving my ambivalent feelings about my parents and moving toward emotional maturity.

Early in my professional career, I realized two things about therapy. First, the patient has to be capable of change. Secondly, it is the personal interaction between doctor and patient that provides the critical spark that can make therapy work. Somehow, Bella and I had this connection from the beginning. Along with meaningful dialogue, the therapist must provide that indefinable something that I have called interest and concern. He or she must also be honest, understanding, warm, and willing to communicate. Therapy cannot fill the void caused by childhood deprivation. However, psychiatric therapy can do much to reconcile the hurt, allow you to leave it behind, gain a perspective and start to move forward. Many patients, who have succeeded in therapy with me, have told me in their own way: "You seemed to care about me." "You made me feel worthwhile for the first time." Perhaps that indefinable something is love.

CHAPTER 6:
THE BOYS OF WARD THREE SOUTH

Starting in November of 1967, my caseload was changed and become more diverse. After four and a half months of just seeing female inpatients, I was also assigned ward three south male patients. Whereas the female ward was chaotic and noisy, the male ward had a quiet and yet menacing atmosphere. Opening the locked door of this unit, you felt as if you were entering a dark foreboding cave where danger lurked. I was often in fear of physical harm. One day, just as I was becoming more comfortable with the ward, the emergency button in the physician's office went off. We ran in to find, Dr. Paul Kaplan, my supervisor and mentor, bleeding from a head wound that he had sustained at the hands of a belligerent patient.

Looking out from the safety of the glass enclosed nursing station as I wrote my chart notes, I could observe the day room. Schizophrenic males roamed the area like tigers on the prowl. At times, they shook their fists angrily at the ceiling responding to inner stimuli or their hallucinations. Some sat around the periphery of the dayroom with blank stares on their faces looking as if they might pounce at any moment. Sometimes, patients would remove their clothes and even masturbate. Fights would break out or patients would bang on the nursing station glass demanding attention. When I first viewed this scene, I stood and stared in amazement. A fellow psychiatric resident expressed it well when he exclaimed, "What the hell have I gotten myself into?"

A welcome break from this frightening patient load was my work with several adolescent patients. These young men struggled with identity issues in different ways. James for instance walked around the ward carrying a law book and told everyone he was going to be an attorney. Sean, a handsome thin seventeen year old , who was admitted due to depression and drug use, wore a heavy white fisherman knit sweater, perhaps to portray a toughness he did not have. John, a short and squat twenty year old, whom we called the poet, carried a book of his writings under his arm. His attitude was one of intellectual superiority.

Sean and John stand out in my mind. Sean had the look of a graceful fawn – delicate, somewhat vulnerable and innocent. His presence somehow caught you off guard and made you wonder how he would survive in our rough and tumble world. He had tried to kill himself three months earlier. He admitted to alcohol and drug dependency including mescaline, codeine and Miltown and living a promiscuous life. He explained his drug use as an effort to fill a void, which he could not fill in any other way. Many years later, I started to use the phrase "The Void" to explain to needy patients why they felt the way that they do. It was not until I wrote the above lines that I realized that I have to attribute the phrase to Sean.

Sean's parents were divorced and each had remarried. He had been shuttled from one parent to another from Europe to the United States. He said that he had recently come to America to live with his father to find himself and to escape the restrictions imposed on him by his stepfather. His mother felt that he was a horrible failure. His father, Dr. Benjamin, a clinical psychologist, professed a desire to help his son but was only willing to give a limited amount of his own time and personal effort. He appeared almost relieved to be able to allow the hospital to take over his parental function.

I worked hard with Sean, during the three months that he was a patient at H.S.H., to help him express his adolescent angst and his anger toward his parents. We talked about many things, including politics, sex, religion, his fears and his sense of inferiority. When he talked of killing himself, I told him that life changes and that if he were not here next Tuesday, he would not know what it had changed into. Often such changes are positive. I tried to foster hope that he would continue to grow, gain more control over his life and go to college to become a foreign correspondent, using his knowledge of French and German to good advantage. I told him that he needed to accept the void that lack of parental nurturing had helped create, not fight it or try to fill it with drugs. He needed to survive and find people and things that made him happy and content.

I discharged him in April and followed him on an outpatient basis until I left Haverford in September to continue my Fellowship. On our last visit, Sean reported that he was attending high school and had gotten a part time job as a stock boy. I was heartbroken to learn two years later that Sean had committed suicide. I want to believe that his stay at Haverford State Hospital had somehow prolonged the inevitable.

John had been an intellectually precocious but autistically withdrawn child. In childhood, he adapted to life by escaping to intellectual pursuits and a world of fantasy. In adolescence, he had trouble dealing with his search for personal identity, erotic themes, the anxiety of the Vietnam War and family health problems. His sister was involved in an auto accident in which she sustained severe facial injuries. Doctors hospitalized his mother on several occasions due to heart problems. His father developed carcinoma of the mouth, became blind in one eye and underwent a radical resection of the jaw.

Now at age 20, having difficulty trying to bridge the gap between adolescence and adulthood and devastated by his father's battle with cancer of the mouth, John had regressed into psychosis.

Upon admission, he stated, "I'm dying. I've forgotten how to sleep. I need blood. I can't live anymore. My poor little heart doesn't feel it can take anymore." When asked about his father's condition, he answered, "I feel guilty that I could not do more for him. He should have been stricter. I was spoiled. It made me a fat person." At new case conference, he answered our questions as follows: "I can't understand English when it is spoken; nothing means anything to me. I have no ego. I don't exist; I always felt rejected; I was fat and people made fun of me." The chief of male services decided on a diagnosis of psychotic depressive reaction in a pre-morbid schizoid personality.

John required constant support from me. When I gave it, he was well oriented and knowledgeable. When it was not available, he regressed to crying spells, offered many physical complaints and had hysterical seizure equivalents, which he called his "spells." He continued to be fearful and asked for constant reassurance. He felt that he was going to die and stated, "I want to die in my sleep." He felt that the nurses were going to kill him and that his medication was poison. Overcome with loneliness and despair, afraid of the responsibility of maturity and laden with guilt, he seemed to drift back to childhood by entering the realm of psychosis.

Having been an English major in college, I tried to relate to him and use his writing in therapy. Upon admission, he presented me with 46 pages of poems and prose vignettes written during the 12-month period prior to his psychotic decompensation. He fantasized himself as a poet with the pen name of Ian Burke, but preferred even in his poems to remain a six-year-old child. John described himself as "a tiny presence struggling for life." I tried in vain to get him to take a risk, try to move forward and follow his dream. He expressed his feelings in a long poem called "yesterday of the mind." The following is one of the paragraphs:

"So today I am fully grown
Having left the teens behind.
I have stared life in the face,
And this is what I find:
The world is for machines,
For the insensitive and blue.
Man is seldom happier than
When he's four and two."

I wondered about my interest in these teenage patients. Of course, their emotional fragility and vulnerability played a part. I wanted to help and make them stronger. I also knew that I had been a lonely child who became a needy moody adolescent myself. At the end of my Fellowship, I had my first journal article published. The title was "adolescent depression." Although I dated and had friends, I was often frustrated, and wanted something more from people- a different level of intimacy and closeness. Later in life, I realized that then, I wanted instant gratification. I also know now that in real life, we get to know people and form friendships gradually, as we piece together the things we find out about them. It was not until at least thirty years later that I connected the dots and realized the final piece of the puzzle. Doing therapy with these young men fulfilled my need for male bonding and gave me a little of the closeness that I had wanted with my own father.

My patients trust me. That has always been one of my strengths as a therapist. They let me in by sharing their lives and much personal material. The relationship with many of my patients still allows me to obtain a level of intimacy in a way that is safe, gratifying and yet allows me to feel in control in my role as a psychiatrist/father figure. This is probably one of the reasons that I was attracted to becoming a psychiatrist in the first place.

On unit Three South, as on all units, we made decisions about patients at new case conference, disposition, or discharge conference in the ward conference room in a group process led by the Clinical Director of Building four. Also present were the Chief of female/ male services, the Unit Chief, the head nurse, and a social worker, a member of the industrial therapy department and a member of the occupational therapy department. They were all dressed in business attire. The hospital did not permit casual dress. We all sat respectfully as a staff or ward physician, such as me, would present the case. The patient would then be called in and interviewed by the Clinical Director as eight to ten sets of eyes, sat quiet but attentive, peering into their soul and scrutinizing their every word and action.

For the most part doctors treated the patients courteously. However, at times, this was not true. One Clinical Director in particular sometimes took liberties that were upsetting for the patient and greatly annoyed me. On one occasion, we were interviewing a male patient. The director noted that the patient had a medical history of Syphilis. He asked the patient if he had any sores on his penis Although the patient answered "No," the Doctor asked him to stand, with his back to us, and drop his pants, in front of every body, so that he could check to be sure. How demeaning and embarrassing this behavior must have been for the patient.

Looking back, I wondered why I did not struggle more with this ethical dilemma. I also wondered why no one including myself spoke to anyone about this inappropriate behavior. The only answer that I can come up with is that it was 1967 and the doctor was king. He or she had complete control over the patient and his word was final. The staff tolerated what he did without question. That is the way it was.

After the patient went back to the ward, a discussion ensued. At new case conference a treatment plan was established. At disposition conference, each service gave their input. We considered factors such as their prior psychiatric history and their number of prior psychiatric hospitalizations. We also reviewed their response to medication and their ability to comply with taking their medication. The nurse reported their responses to a home visits, if any. Social service discussed placement issues, such as the availability of family support and alternative places to live. After this, the Clinical Director decided if the patient could be safely discharged or placed on trail visit to live in the community or if they instead required additional treatment in a closed or open setting at the hospital. All my patients, including Sean, John, Loretta and Bella went thought this process.

Chapter 7:
Loss, Guilt and Depression

The months after Bella went home on her trial visit was a time of loss for both of us. My Father died on May 27, 1968, at age fifty-seven, of non-Hodgkin's lymphoma. His death left me with a huge wound filled with ambivalent feelings involving affection, anger and guilt that took me years to understand, resolve and heal. My main regret was that we never got the chance to become closer. Although the doctors made the official diagnosis, while I was in my internship in Columbus, Ohio in 1966, his illness probably began in 1941, just months after I was born.

At that time, at age thirty-three, my father became very ill. The doctors did not know what was wrong with him. Because his spleen swelled, the doctors had to remove it. Following the surgery, his skin and the whites of his eyes yellowed. His gallbladder became inflamed. They said that his prognosis was poor. The family story is that when they discharged him from the hospital, we moved in with my maternal grandparents, where Bubba Paul nursed him back to health. My father's family dealt with his illness in their own way. They were orthodox Jews and believed that according to the Talmud (Rosh Hashanah 16B), if you changed the Hebrew first name of the very sick person that the angel of death would be unable to find him. Thus my father, Fivish (Frank), in a solemn formal ceremony in the synagogue, requiring a minyan constituting a quorum of ten men, became Shraga Fivish. Whether it was my grandmother's nurturing or his rebirth fostered by the name change, the evil decree averted and he recovered. Whatever his malady, it probably went into remission and I had a father in my life for another twenty-five years.

In February of 1965, his illness probably returned. After a bad cold, he discovered an enlarged lymph node under his jawbone. That summer, he saw several physicians. Their opinions varied from a stone blocking the salivary duct, to lymphosarcoma, a type of cancer. In September, he had a biopsy. The doctor sent a tissue sample to the Armed Forces Institute of Pathology. They reported that since no 'Reed-Sternberg cells' were found, he did not have Hodgkin's disease. Instead, they suggested the possibility of a protein disorder or an atypical disorder of the parotid gland.

The above made little impact on me. I was newly married, immersed in my last year of medical training and making plans for my internship year. At the end of June of 1966, I drove my very pregnant wife, sitting on a pillow in the passenger seat, up and down the hills of Virginia, with a small trailer attached to the car containing our worldly possessions. Our destination was Columbus, Ohio where I would begin my one-year rotating internship at Doctors Hospital on July 1st. As was their style, my parents protected me and shared very little of the medical news or their anxiety concerning my father's condition so as not to interfere with my professional studies.

In October, someone hit our car during the night as it sat in front of the intern's quarters. My father wrote me a chatty short letter detailing what I had to do to handle the insurance situation. He asked about my wife and our new baby. In passing, at the end of the letter, he matter-of-factly stated, "Enclosed are the reports I told you about. Show them to the pathologist at your hospital and I am sure that he will be interested. Love and Kisses, Daddy." At the time, I thought nothing of it. However, looking back, the calmness of his words astonishes me. That was my father!

His life went on. He continued to function at top capacity as a good soldier. He persisted to work full time, quietly fulfill his philanthropic duties and be there for his family and extended family for another twenty months. By that time, I had returned to the Philadelphia area to start my Fellowship in Psychiatry. One day, he asked me to go to his office with him. This was an unusual request. We were there for about two hours as he finished various files on his desk. He gave me some nominal tasks to do to keep me busy that I do not remember. What I do remember is untangling and separating many paper clips in a glass dish. Neither of us said a word, but I sensed that he wanted me there with him.

Later that day, after we left his office, he walked several blocks to pick up some cakes that he knew his sister liked and hand delivered them to her. The next day, he entered the hospital. From the minute that he lay down in that hospital bed, he seemed to change from the strong independent man that I knew to a shrunken, pale-skinned man who did not complain as the nurses fussed over him and inserted a catheter. It was as if he had pushed himself to finish what he could before he gave in to the illness.

Several days later, I received a phone call from my wife at work telling me that my Father had been moved to the intensive care unit. I drove from Haverford State Hospital to Albert Einstein Hospital in South Philadelphia, with my adrenalin pumping. The ride seemed to take forever. When I got there, I stood at the door of the intensive care unit, completely frozen and feeling helpless. Although I could clearly see him lying in bed, I was unable to move my feet through the door. The next day, my father-in-law took me back and pushed me through the door. I have no recollection of this or of my last conversation with my father. Later that day, he held my mother's hand and thanked her for being his wife. He died that night. It was Monday, May 27, 1968. He was 57. I was 27.

I was upset, irritable and had an angry look on my face throughout the funeral. I was particularly annoyed with his family. At the time, like my mother, I blamed them for being one of the forces that took him away from me during my childhood. I told them, "you took him away from me and now I will never have him." It was not until many years later that I understood that it had been his choice to be the helpful patriarch of his family and busy himself with charity organizations. These activities fulfilled his needs and made him happy. After my mother died, I went through a photo album of pictures from his organizational work. There he was wearing a funny hat and laughing. I had never seen this side of my Father.

Within fourteen months, after my father died, Bella would be dealing with her own sorrow and family crisis. In December, the Doctors Hammond discharged Bella from Haverford State Hospital on a trial visit and sent her home to her parent's house in Springfield, Pennsylvania. However, as she had done many times before, during childhood and adolescence, after a few days, she left and went to her maternal grandparent's house in Drexel Hill, Delaware County, Pennsylvania.

For the next eight months, things went well. Bella lived mostly in her Grandparent's house, but would sleep over from time to time at her parents' house, which was approximately five miles away. Here she would spend time with her younger siblings, Mary Kay, Ann and Luke who still lived at home. She worked part-time for the Manpower Temporary Agency doing typing. She dated a young man named Larry from the Lake Carey, Pennsylvania area. Her Grandmother, who felt they would be perfect together, had introduced her to him. Grandma liked him because he was Catholic. She had pegged him as a future in-law. Her Grandparents wanted a summer home away from the city, which could also serve as a safe house in the event of nuclear war. They settled in Lake Carey, Pennsylvania, outside of Scranton, 165 miles from Philadelphia. They used the home during the summer months. During the winter, they rented the Lake Carey house to Larry, who also acted as a caretaker.

On July 21, 1968, the world exploded for Bella. Her Brother Will, intoxicated and driving on Route 352 near route 3 and 926, on the way to the movies, died instantly, when he hit another auto going around a bad curve. Their sister, Mary Kay and a female friend were in the car. Although severely injured, they survived the crash. Will had joined the marines when he finished high school. He was home on leave from active duty in Viet Nam at the time of the crash. Bella's grief was overwhelming. She could not sleep, paced the halls and cried.

Over the course of the next 19 days, Bella deteriorated further emotionally. She returned to Haverford State Hospital from her trial visit on August 9, 1968. Admissions had again assigned her to my service, in building four on ward three north. That morning, I came into the nursing station and Nurse Mary told me that I had two new patients that had come in during the night. One was a fifty-four year old man who had a chronic brain syndrome due to Alcoholism. He also was paranoid, thinking that the neighbors were stealing his things. Twelve days later, after he was stabilized, he was transferred "down the hill." to the geriatric unit. The other patient was Bella. Although, I was surprised to hear her name again, I was not shocked. Recidivism or relapse was common. Later that morning, I led her into the doctor's office for an interview. She seemed fragile but was not as bizarre or as agitated as she had been when I first met her the year before. She walked slowly, sat down and closed her eyes. When she did talk, her words came out slowly, but her mind seemed clear and her associations were coherent and relevant.

"So Bella," I said, "we are here again. What happened?"
She looked at me and through a veil of tears, said, "Will is dead."

There was much evidence of guilt and depressive ideas. She said, "My brother died last month. I was supposed to go (to the movies with them) but I changed my mind at the last minute. I was very close to him. Two weeks before, I had bought him a bottle of Seagram's

Seven as a gift because he had brought me home cigarettes from the service. He died in a car accident. He was drinking rye whiskey."

Bella looked thin but was neatly dressed as usual. She was accessible but frequently became irritated with herself because of her re-admission to the hospital. At times, she answered my questions in a flat depressed tone. She trembled and her muscles tensed. I could sense her fear.

Her orientation and memory were within normal range. She was able to read and understand a newspaper article that I gave her to read. She was able to subtract serial 7's.

Bella was delusional. She indicated that after her brother's death that her mother would not leave her alone. "She tried to draw me to her with the suction of the fan. I could not stand it. I felt as if I was burning up inside. She was standing on the steps. It looked like my mother but she was wearing a mask and looked like the devil."

When asked, she admitted having auditory hallucinations. She indicated that the voices were that of the devil and said "no-stop-go."

She knew that Lyndon Johnson was the president of the United States and could tell me a few current news events. She was able to abstract proverbs but her responses reflected her present situation. In response to the Meat Poison Proverb, she indicated, "one may be able to take something and one may not be able to take it."

She had some insight. She realized that she was upset and needed help. I felt that her judgment was impaired due to psychotic thoughts.

This time, my diagnostic impression was Schizophrenia, Schizo-Affective Type, depressed type. 295.74

Things had not changed much since Bella's last visit to building four. The patient mix on ward three north still contained patients suffering from paranoid schizophrenia, organic brain disorders, and various depressive reactions. Nurse Mary was still writing nursing notes and dispensing medications. The aids were taking blood pressures and pulses and trying to keep order in the chaos. A significant change was that Brenda was gone. Another patient had taken over the piano on three north and often played the same song over and over which drove the nurses wild. As Bella reconstituted, she also would often go into the day room and play chopsticks repeatedly to aggravate the nursing staff.

In the months that Bella was away from the hospital, rather than mourning the death of my father, I plunged further into my psychiatric training. Diagnostic categories changed. I had to remember that Psychoneurotic Disorders were now called Neuroses. I had to keep in mind new terms such as neurasthenic neurosis and depersonalization neurosis. The term sociopathic personality disturbance was no loner acceptable. Its subheadings, of addiction and sexual deviation had become separate diagnoses. There was so much to learn.

After one week, on the closed unit, Bella was calmer. Her worries, fears and doubts had diminished. She was less depressed, had stopped crying, and was no longer delusional. The staff considered her well enough for transfer back to building 12. Her stay there was uneventful. Six weeks later, on September 27, 1968, Dr. Hammond discharged her to go home.

A few weeks after my father's death, my daughter, my wife and I attended a Haverford State Hospital staff picnic at Rose Twig Camp in the Pocono Mountains of Pennsylvania. The camp owner had a beautiful brown and white dog. When our daughter saw him, she started to scream. Six months earlier, she had been scared when a neighbor's dog had jumped on her. To pacify her, the owner showed us the dog's new litter of puppies. Our daughter stopped crying and began to play with the puppies. One in particular, a pure white puppy, caught her fancy. We told the camp owner the story of what had happened in December. He said that although he had not planned to break up the litter, that he would give the little white dog to us. Our daughter was thrilled. We named him Haverford. He was a frisky little ball of white and served as a distraction for me. Three months later, we got an eviction notice. Apparently, soon after we moved in, the landlord changed the apartment bylaws. Although he would allow dogs to stay that already occupied the building, he would not allow any new dogs. Haverford had to go. At the end of September, we gave our puppy Haverford away to a friend, Bella went home, and I left Haverford State Hospital to begin my two years of out- patient training. We all said goodbye and started a new phase of our life.

CHAPTER 8:
BOB AND BELLA-THE ROAD TO RECOVERY

Things were quieter at the Devlin home this time when Bella returned home. Her parents, subdued by Will's death were a little kinder to her. She still lived mostly at her grandparents' house. Her mother bugged her about doing more socially. One day, in early January of 1969, her friend Betsy talked about a dance scheduled at the Delaware County Community College in Concordville, Pennsylvania. Mrs. Devlin encouraged her to go. At the dance, Bella met a 20-year-old West Chester College Junior, an education major, named Bob. His sister, a student at the College had told him about the function. Dressed casually in Kakis and a blue button down shirt, Bob came to the dance with three male friends. Bob was attracted to this pretty petite girl with platinum blond hair and big blue eyes. They shared a soda and he asked her to dance. They talked and agreed to go to Maras Pizza in Springfield Township, Delaware County with Betsy and his friends. She was very sarcastic to his friends and he was somehow impressed by this behavior. He got her phone number and called her the following week for a date.

A week later, on their first date, they went downtown to Philadelphia to see the movie, "Finnegan's Rainbow." Bella was extremely nervous. She would not talk about her family but did tell Bob that she had a marine brother, who had just been killed in an automobile accident. She also mentioned that she had a sister who was mentally ill but would not share any details about her. One of the things that Bob and Bella had in common was their knowledge of the Lake Carey, Pennsylvania area. Her Grandmother had a summer home in Lake Carey and Bob had two uncles who had stores in Scranton and a great uncle who lived in the area. After their date, he took her home to her Grandmother's house and kissed her on the cheek. She later told him that she thought it was very sweet and liked it that he was a gentleman. They made plans to see each other again.

While I was at the Philadelphia Mental Health Clinic, doing my outpatient Fellowship training, Bella and Bob continued to date. Bob finished college and Bella got a full time job as a secretary. Bob had told her that he would not continue to date her unless she got a full time job. They listened to Peter, Paul & Mary and the Beatles. They read and discussed Mario Puzo's book <u>The Godfather</u> and Philip Roth's <u>Portnoy's Complaint</u>. They saw Paul Newman and Robert Redford in "Butch Cassidy and the Sundance Kid" and Dustin Hoffman in "Midnight Cowboy."

The Devlin family continued to be intimidating and frightening to Bob. He would bring Bella home to the family house and find her father waiting on the front steps, intoxicated and angry that they were fifteen minutes late. Bella's mother would invite wounded veterans to the house in hopes that they could find a mate for their daughters. Her mother would flirt, hug the service men and compete with her daughters for the young men's attention. She never hugged Bob. She talked about one of her neighbors as "those Jews" and remarked in front of Bob that like her mother, she wanted Bella to marry a Catholic man. Bella, however, told him that she liked Jewish men.

As the decade of the 1960's drew to a close, the hippie generation burst onto the national consciousness. Teens embraced the counterculture emphasizing sexual freedom and drug experimentation. Haight-Asbury flourished on the West Coast in San Francisco and 400,000 people gathered for the Woodstock festival near Bethel, New York. Bella remained naive and oblivious to it all. She continued to see her friend Madrilène from Haverford State Hospital. One day, Bella drove Madrilène and her boyfriend to meet another friend at an apartment house at 63rd and Walnut Streets in Philadelphia. In the car, they asked Bella if she smoked. She answered that she smoked Salem cigarettes and they laughed. Bella did not get the joke. The four of them went up to the roof to relax. The friend had drugs and the three of them proceeded to shoot up. Bella was horrified and left. She never saw Madrilène again.

Prior to dating Bella, Bob had dated a young woman who ended up going into a convent. Bob was "exclusive" from the day he met Bella. He assumed that Bella was also only seeing him. She was not and continued to date others. One day, late in the summer, he drove Bella to the bus depot so that she could visit her grandmother in Lake Carey. She admitted that she was going to see her boyfriend. He was very hurt. For Christmas of 1969, Bob gave Bella a friendship ring that he had purchased from his uncle's jewelry store in Scranton. It was a gold ring with a diamond chip that was worth 3-400 dollars. He had been able to purchase it for $75.00. Her family congratulated them on their engagement. Bella and Bob were both embarrassed. They made it plain that it was just a gift. The family continued to tease them about it.

Bella's mother talked about Bella's mental health problems and tried to discourage Bob from coming around. Bella's psychiatric history did not stop him. He had heard of Haverford State Hospital. He told Bella about his first experience with H.S.H. "When I was in high school my best friend's mother was a patient at Haverford State. One day, he asked me to drive him to H.S.H. to see his mother. I dropped him off in front of building four, waited and then drove him home. He made me promise that I wouldn't tell anybody that his mother was there. He wouldn't tell me why she was there or what the deal was. It was scary the way he acted. I felt that he over reacted." Bella and Bob often talked about the stigma of mental illness. Bob felt that Bella was remarkable that she just made up her mind to forget it and just go on.

However, as they continued to date, and he fell more in love, he sometimes had second thoughts. He worried that Bella would get emotionally ill again and have to be rehospitalized. He told his best friend, "I can't back out now. What would she do with out me? I provide this positive influence in her life. She finally has someone whom she can depend on and who can provide the emotional support that she needs to keep her from going over the edge. I'm someone who can take care of her. Sometimes I feel trapped. Sometimes I feel that I have no choice and that it is my responsibility. How could I live with myself if I didn't do these things for her.?"

As Bob and Bella continued to date and get to know each other better, I moved forward in my training to satisfy the two-year outpatient requirement to complete my fellowship in psychiatry.

Chapter 9:

Philadelphia Mental Health Clinic

In 1968, there were few facilities where an Osteopathic Physician could get training in Psychiatry. In the early 1960's, Floyd Dunn, D.O. learned that the U.S. Government was giving grant money for continuing medical education and started the first Osteopathic Training Program in Psychiatry at the Kansas City College of Osteopathic Medicine. Cecil Harris, D.O. subsequently opened the first psychiatric training center for Osteopathic Physicians on the east coast at the Philadelphia Mental Health Clinic, through a grant from the National Institute of Mental Health (N.I.M.H.). The clinic's advisory committee included such notables as Pearl S. Buck, Theodor Reik, Ph.D. and Francis Strawbridge, Jr.

When I started my outpatient training, the clinic occupied a three story stone row house at 935 Pine Street in the historic section of Philadelphia. The front door opened into a small vestibule. From here, you went through a second door into a long hallway and faced the stairs. To your left was a door, which led into a cheerless 8'x12' waiting room with a secretarial area at the back. The stairway leading upstairs was dim and foreboding. At the top was an equally dark long hall with several former bedrooms that were now used as trainee offices. The fellows in training went into their offices and closed the doors leaving the hallway subdued and empty. The third floor contained additional offices with a similar facade. Somehow, the overall physical and emotional character of the mental health clinic including the dark hallways and the perpetually closed doors on the second and third floors resembled my childhood home and reawakened the feelings of loneliness and isolation that I had felt as a child.

I grew up from age 3 to 12 in a semi-detached brick house, in Philadelphia, on the edge of what is now called Northern Liberties. Here also you entered into a vestibule and through a second door down a long dark hallway to the stairs. The front room was used as a combination home office for my father and a den for the family. In the back of the house were a living room, dining room and kitchen. There must have been activity in the house but all I remember is the silence and the dim light. I remember entering the house and looking through the French doors that boarded the hallway to see if my father was home. If I had to go upstairs, I moved quickly scared of the darkness. At the top of the stairs was a landing. To your right was a bathroom followed by our three bedrooms. To your left, you walked up several steps to another landing in front of a door that led to a two-room rental apartment that shared our bathroom. Up a narrow stairway, in the attic was a second two room and bath rental apartment.

Except for watching boxing, my father voiced no interest in sports. I did not play little league baseball or soccer. There were no children on my block, except for two girls across the streets, who were a little older than I was. I spent my time at home mostly in solitary play with crayons and plastic soldiers. In the small back yard, I collected grasshoppers in a jar and kept my eye on a perpetually pregnant cat that had taken up residence in our shed. My father was often out of the house. Occasionally, my mother would drive me to see a classmate in a different neighborhood. My parents valued a good education. Therefore I did not attend the neighborhood public school but walked from Seventh and Brown streets to Broad and Spring Garden streets, a distance of about ten blocks, to attend the Thaddeus Stevens School of Practice (an elementary school), where they trained teachers.

As a small boy, I remember hesitantly knocking on the closed doors of the two rental apartments seeking companionship. The first apartment housed a married couple, Mr. and Mrs. Herbert, who at that time were probably middle aged. Mr. Herbert would have me sit on his lap and read me the comics from the "Philadelphia Bulletin." The Whites lived in the attic apartment. They very seldom went out. They seemed older. She had severe rheumatoid arthritis with deformed hands that were scary to a youngster. However, on some days in desperate need for human contact, I would climb the narrow stairs to their small den like dwelling, to visit them. At the time, these four adults were my friends and parent surrogates.

There were seven training Fellows in my group at the clinic who varied in age, from 28 to probably 40. We all had different backgrounds. At 28, I was one of the youngest. At that time, my interpersonal skills were limited and I often felt apart from the group. Looking back, we probably had little in common except for our desire to become psychiatrists. It was a stressful time. We were learning Freudian concepts that were new to us. Like second year medical students or college psychology majors, we tended to see ourselves in many of the disorders that we studied. We spent a lot of time kidding around and using our new analytical knowledge to analyze each other. We listened to each other gripe and reviewed the assigned material together. We helped each other get though the stressful rite of passage called residency training. I felt closest to one of the Fellows, Dr. Hank, who was my age and had been a classmate of mine in medical school.

We had five different supervisors who also had different backgrounds. Some had received their trained in California in an analytical training center that at that time would take Osteopathic Physicians. Some had taken five years of training in Neurology and Psychiatry. Hence, the name of our national organization, at that time, was The American College of Neuropsychiatrists. Their supervision styles varied from the mostly non-verbal approach common among analysts to one psychiatrist who took a group of us to Schraft's Restaurant for lunch to discuss psychiatric outpatient practice. We read and reread such tomes as Ernest Jones' <u>Papers on Psychoanalysis</u>, <u>The Writings of Anna Freud: The Ego and the Mechanisms of Defense</u> and Peter Blos', <u>On Adolescence: A Psychoanalytic Interpretation</u>.

At other times, we sat on the chairs or floor of the waiting room to hear lectures on various topics such as dreams interpretation, personality disorder dynamics, neurotic and psychotic symptoms, and adolescent behavior. In between, we saw outpatients and had supervision. A special treat was our attendance on Tuesday afternoons from 1-3 PM at neurology grand rounds at a local allopathic hospital. It was unheard of for an Osteopathic Physician to attend. However, one of our doctors was friends with the neurologist who ran this conference and was able to obtain entry for us. On Saturday, we attended the psychoanalytic studies institute where we had continuous adult case study, lectures on the theory of neurosis and group therapy dynamics.

Dr. Edythe Gates Varner, Chairman, Department of Neuropsychiatry, was my most memorable supervisor. I looked forward to supervision with her on Thursday from 1-2 PM. She was a tall, gangly women who wore long earrings, which she explained defined her femininity. Her style was quiet and reserved. However, she was very perceptive. She could sense my anxiety underneath my calm façade. She was the first female authority figure to give me a compliment. One day, while we were discussing one of my patients, she said, "You are very insightful. The patients trust you." This praise made me glow and did much for my professional self-esteem. In her quiet way, she was a wonderful role model. She taught me things about patients and the nuances of therapy, which I have carried with me throughout my professional career.

At the time, I was treating a borderline personality disorder named Stan. He was 6'2" tall and weighed 250 lbs. His main affect was anger. He had superior intelligence but could not use it in a way that would be helpful to him in life. Because he looked like a vagrant, I affectionately called him "Stan the Bag Lady." Every session, he came into the room carrying a large umbrella. He enjoyed walking around the room during the session swinging the umbrella in an intimidating fashion and asking me questions about engineering, which he knew a lot about but about which I knew nothing. I sat clutching the arms of the chair trying to not show my fear that he would harm me physically.

One day, Dr. Varner said to me "Why do you think he acts that way? How do you think he feels that he has to act that way?" It had not dawned on me before. The answer was that he felt inadequate and was afraid of me! Secure people do not act this way. This helped me calm down and put things in perspective. Gradually, as I became kinder and less anxious, Stan stopped prancing and sat in the chair. His anger diminished.

Joe was a twenty-seven year old who suffered from obsessive-compulsive symptoms. Usually passive, he could not understand why he suddenly would think of killing people. He could not get the thoughts out of his head. Sometimes counting to one hundred helped but usually the anxiety persisted. He often had a need to check that he had locked his apartment and car doors. He abhorred dirt. He washed his hands and showered often. In spite of these distractions, he had friends, a good job and was involved in many activities.

As I was being trained to do, I listened carefully to his story and asked him many questions about his childhood, parents and adolescence. My goal was to grow up with him again to see how he had become the man that he was. In therapy, I as able to educate him about his disorder and reassure him that he was not alone. Our rapport was good. He seemed comforted by my interest and concern. Slowly, we were able to trace his conflict back to toilet training. Joe was even able to remember the white tiles of his childhood bathroom. I prescribed him a tranquilizer, which helped him reduce his anxiety, relax and cope better. However, no matter how hard I worked, his obsessive-compulsive symptoms continued. In spite of this, Joe kept coming back. One day, I complained to Dr. Varner that I did not feel that I was doing enough for Joe. Her insightful answer was, "you don't know what you mean to the patient. Just being there and listening means a lot."

It would take 20 years before psychiatry could offer Joe more. Looking back, I wish that I had many of the psychiatric medications available today to treat my clinic patients in 1968. However, my training at the time clearly showed me the benefits possible from the doctor patient relationship that is individual psychotherapy. Many of the trainees at the PMHC went into analysis. Thinking that it would be helpful to see how it felt to be on the other side of the desk, I followed the herd and entered a training analysis.

CHAPTER 10:
CHANGE AND TURMOIL

The early nineteen seventies was a time of change and turmoil in the United States of America. The flower children rose up and men started to let their hair grow long. The Chicago conspiracy trial, found Abbie Hoffman and six other defendants not guilty of plotting to incite a riot in the 1968 democratic convention. Thousands of gay men and women marched from New York's Greenwich Village to Central Park to assert gay pride and solidarity. The Vietnam War continued. Campus unrest became common as students rose up in opposition to the war. The Kent State Shootings shocked the nation. In 1972, the courts indicted seven men in the Watergate Break-in. Finally, on January 27, 1973, a cease-fire went into effect in Vietnam. President Nixon, faced with impeachment, became the first American President to resign, when he stepped down from office on August 8, 1974.

These years were also a time of change and turmoil for Bella and me. Bob and Bella got married, the government drafted Bob and I was in my training analysis. Many of the trainees at the PMHC went into psychoanalysis with Dr. Morris Isaac. Being naive, I trusted the recommendation without any personal research. I later found out that he was not a physician. He had received his analytic training at the Berlin Institute and subsequently got a Ph.D. in the Philippines. Our relationship began with me driving, what seemed a long distance, to Berwyn, Pennsylvania so that he could see me three mornings a week at 7:30 AM (not my best time of day) before he started his employment at the Devereux Foundation. I paid him $20.00 a session. My time on the couch was spend feeling anxious and complaining about my childhood memories of my mother's self centeredness and lack of affection and my Aunt Cheryl's overly sensual displays of affection and endearment that scared me as a youth. When I look back and remember these sessions, it seems strange to me that he never once asked me about my father who had died less than two years before.

Dr. Isaac offered me no interpretation about my anger. He just let me rant. My anger toward my Father was submerged. It had showed itself only through the palpable tension between us. It did not start to come to the surface until after he died. I finally understood it clearly much later in my life with the help of another therapist. My anger toward my Mother was right below the surface. It took very little provocation for it to come out. One day in my thirties, after my Mother had remarried, I remember becoming furious with her and running out of her apartment. I went back a few minutes later. Her new husband said, "You know your Mother loves you." His insight startled me. I did not know this simple fact.

One day several years later, I was driving my Mother to the cemetery to visit my Father's grave, as I always did at the time of the Jewish New Year. I had been thinking about it for a while and decided to confront her. "Mom," I said, "Why don't you ever tell me that you love me?" She tensed up and answered, "Why don't you tell me that? What do you want me to do, shout it like Aunt Cheryl does and grab you and hug the kiskas (guts) out of you like she does?" I did not answer and just kept driving. I thought to myself, "Something in the middle might be nice." I also realized that in my anger, I held back and did not tell her that I loved her. I started to try.

I often wondered why my Mother always frustrated me so and was continually able to engender such an atypical anger response. It was not until I was editing this book, several years after she died, that the insight came to me. My Mother was not cruel or critical like Bella's but she did something that engendered in me the same irritability that Bella expressed. My Mother's inability to show affection and her avoidance of touch pushed me away emotionally and left me feeling unloved. Her defensive protective wall was like a giant steel door that I had seen when my Father, an attorney, took me with him, as a child, to see a client at Eastern State Penitentiary in Philadelphia. I kept knocking at the door and became more and more frustrated when she would not let me in. I kept acting as if she had what I wanted and would not give it to me. The truth was that she was limited and really did not have it to give in the way that I wanted. After 11 months under Dr. Isaac's mostly nonverbal gaze, I was tired and frustrated running anxiously through this silent analytic maze, with no guidance or direction. Needing more structure, I finally took charge to find an exit route. I stood up and told him that I had had it and would not continue on the couch. At my suggestion, I continued in individual psychotherapy sitting up in a chair rather than prostrate on the couch. Rather than seeing him three times a week, I went to one session per week. This lasted for 5 1/2 more months, mostly at his home office. Although I felt more secure and more in control upright, I mostly spent my sessions crying or verbalizing frustration with those in my childhood life and apparently getting more and more depressed. He must have spoken at times, but I can never remember him saying anything positive or helpful. Mostly, he looked at me through his fingers that he made into a triangle in front of his face.

An analyst friend of mine, years later, told me that tears equate to feelings of anger. Based on this premise, I must have been furious at Dr. Isaac, and I realized much later on, at my father. One day, I came into Dr. Isaac's basement office to find him talking endearingly in German to someone on the phone in tender loving tones. It seemed staged to me at the time. It upset me terribly. My heart raced and I clenched my fists but said nothing. He had hit a nerve leading directly to my sense of neediness for attention and affection. He never commented. Much later, I realized that when I was a child, my father's lack of patience, irritability and physical punishment seemed as irrational to me as Dr. Isaac's behavior throughout my therapy. They both caused me emotional pain with subsequent feelings of helplessness and inadequacy. These submerged emotions produced feelings of anger that would stay with me for a long time. I saw my father so many times give attention to others. I felt that my mother was limited in her ability to show emotion. However, he apparently had something to give. Why didn't he give to me?

My sessions with Dr. Isaac also affected me outside of the therapy room. I served a rotation at Eastern State School and Hospital, Trevose, Pennsylvania for case conferences in child psychiatry. Here, I saw adolescents being treated in cottage like settings and autistic children being "treated" with cattle prods in the main building. One spring day, I was driving down route 611, facing the sun, with two lanes of traffic in each direction. I was preoccupied. Therapy often made me more ruminative and distracted. Blinded by the sun, I suddenly found myself driving toward the on coming traffic having some how crossed the midline. I cannot remember any thing else. However, the cars must have swerved out of my way because my car was not damaged. The next memory I have is sitting in the Eastern State's resident's lounge with my friend, Dr. Hank, anxiously hovering over me. Someone was watching over me that day. Unlike Bella's brother, Will, I was not hurt. However, it was a wake up call. Soon thereafter, after sixteen months under Dr. Isaac's care, and 87 unpleasant sessions, I left therapy feeling frustrated, confused, angry, unfulfilled and disappointed.

During this time, Bob and Bella continued to date. They went to the movies, went out to dinner, and visited with her grandmother. They attended family picnics and hiked in the Tyler Arboretum, outside of Media, Pennsylvania. They enjoyed taking walks during which they talked about life and family. Bob was constantly amazed that her family was so different from his. He felt that they were selfish, whereas he saw his family as loving and supportive. After receiving a B.S. degree in education from Westchester University in June of 1970, Bob taught social studies at Penn Crest High School. Although it was obvious to all that Bob and Bella loved each other, a marriage proposal did not come easily. Bob kept dragging his feet. After they had dated for about a year, Bob told Bella that he was not sure that he wanted a permanent relationship. He went away to visit his uncle in Louisiana for a week. When he came back, her grandmother and her uncle brought back the parakeet and the cage that he had given Bella as a gift. They told him to stay away from Bella.

Bob found out later that while he was away, Bella had tried to harm herself because she felt Bob was cutting off their relationship. She took an overdose of pills. An ambulance took her to Delaware County Hospital. What he did not realize was that she was also reacting to the death of her Grandfather, who had died the month before. She also still missed her Brother Will, although it was two years since a car accident had killed him. One of the reasons that Bella was attracted to Bob was that he reminded her in mannerism and looks of her brother. The thought of Bob's leaving was the final straw. She could not take another loss.

Bob called her and they continued to date. However, he kept telling her that he might not want to get married. "Why bother getting married and having kids." He often said, "I have nieces and nephews. I want to travel with my friends." In February of 1970, Bella gave Bob an ultimatum. He immediately replied that he wanted to be with her and did want to get married. They were officially engaged. During the summer of 1970, they went on a five-day car trip together to New England. Things seemed to be going well.

A complication arose. In December of 1970, the Army drafted Bob and he went to Fort Jackson, South Carolina. Once he was finished with eight weeks of basic training, he was able to come home on weekends unless he was on duty. He also came home for Christmas for 10 days. At the beginning of February of 1971, Bella once again started to put pressure on Bob to get married. She told him that other men were interested in her. However, she said that she wanted to marry him. She did not care where he was going to be stationed or if she was allowed to be there. She would go anyway. Bob however was still hesitant. He did not want the responsibility and worried about her mental state. He knew that she had had emotional problems before. His own father told him to beware of what he was getting into. He also remembered Bella's mother telling him two years before that Bella had a lot of problems.

As usual, Bella got her way. The wedding date was set for May 8, 1971. Bella got busy planning a wedding. Her Mother did not help her with the wedding because she was peeved that Bella had left the family home, ran away to the Buck Hill Hotel and then subsequently moved in with her Grandmother. Bella did not realize that there was another reason for her mother not getting involved. Her parents probably were having financial problems at the time. Bella's father had recently lost his supervisory status at Smith Kline and French due to downsizing. He refused to take any other position but instead took a severance package and left the company. He had grandiose plans of buying a marina. He started his own construction business but he was not making any money.

Once she became engaged, Bella moved out of her grandmother's house and got an apartment in Media, where she had been working as a legal secretary. Bob and Bella argued about where they should be married. Bella had been raised Catholic but was ambivalent about her religion and had left the Catholic Church. For the last three years, she had been attending an Episcopalian Church in Media. She had a friend that was a parishioner there and her maternal grandfather was Episcopalian. Bob's father had been Jewish but did not practice his religion. His mother was a Christian but did not go to church. Bob liked the traditional aspects of Judaism that his family did celebrate and felt close to his family because of this. Bella admired Jewish people and always felt that Jewish men were respectful and had positive virtues. She was also attracted to Bob because she thought that Jewish men did not drink. After growing up with an alcoholic father, she liked the fact that Bob did not drink.

In the end, it was decided, mostly by Bella, that they would have a church wedding at Christ Episcopal Church in Media. She made the invitations herself on a MTST machine (a precursor to the computer that worked with cards).The reception in the church hall for about seventy-five people cost $400.00. Bob and his four ushers wore tuxedos. Bella wore a white wedding gown and veil. Her father walked her down the isle. One of Bob's cousins in a full beard and an afro hairdo walked Bella's mother down the isle. Four bridesmaids and the maid of honor wore print flowered gowns. The church auxiliary provided tea sandwiches. Bella's grandmother paid for the wedding cake and the wine for a toast. They rented wine glasses at a store in Media. After the reception, Bob's family invited all their family to his brother's house for lunch of sandwiches and other light fare.

Bob and Bella went to Brigantine, New Jersey for their honeymoon. They stayed in her Uncle's house at her Grandmother's suggestion. They were supposed to stay five days. On day two, Bob got sick due to some food that he had eaten. On day three, the water main in Brigantine broke and they did not have any water in the house. They cut the trip short and left. They went home to her grandmother's house, packed up and moved to Columbia, South Carolina where Bob had rented a trailer mobile home for them to live in.

On the way to South Carolina, he could not remember if the mobile home was rented furnished. When they arrived, there was no electric or gas because Bob had forgotten to tell the landlord that they were coming early. Bella was scared. However, they laughed and saw it as an adventure that would be exciting. They enjoyed living there. Bob worked as a clerk typist for army community services. Bella got a job working for a reform synagogue in Columbia as a secretary. After six months, she decided to quit and got a job as a legal secretary. The law firm was very impressed with her efficient work. When Bob was done his time in the service, they wanted her to stay and even promised to find Bob a job. Bob wanted to return to the Philadelphia area. Bella said that 650 miles away from her family was not far enough. However, they did return to the East coast because Bob was close to his family and he had a teaching job waiting for him.

In the summer of 1971, Bob got orders that he would be sent to Korea, which was a nondependent zone. Bella panicked. It would be a thirteen-month tour of duty. She would not be able to go with him. He had heard that a deferment was possible on emotional grounds. They formulated a plan. They would call Dr. Hammond, Bella's old psychiatrist friend from Haverford State hospital and ask him to write a letter on their behalf. However, when they called, Dr. Anna told them that Dr. Bruce had retired and was no longer in active practice.

When Dr. Hammond was not able to help them, they called me. I saw Bob and Bella, in my new Merion Park home office, in a converted small-enclosed porch. Bob brought a little chair in from the waiting room. I remembered Bella, but I had not seen her since she left Haverford State Hospital. Her blond hair was a little shorter and worn in a conservative bob. She was dressed neatly and conservatively in white slacks and a red sweater set with white dots. She sat down and immediately went into assertive mode pressing me hard to write a letter that would explain that she was unable to survive on her own without Bob. I hardly had a chance to say hello.

Years later, Bob confided in me that he had once been hesitant to call me when Bella need hospitalization because he felt that I had been reluctant to write this letter, because I felt that Bella and he were trying to pull a fast one. Thinking back, I probably did feel a little manipulated, but remembering and accepting Bella's forceful streak, I discounted her behavior and wrote the letter anyway based on her serious psychiatric history. In a two-page letter, I reiterated some of Bella's psychiatric record including her suicide attempt in 1970. I wrote that in interview she had stated, "I wish I was dead… If anything happened to Bobby, I would go into a convent…I'm afraid. I have no one except Bobby. My parents have rejected me. ..My grandfather died in September of 1970 and my grandmother is elderly. Sometimes, I get depressed and carried away. I'm worried that it could possibly happen again." I concluded, "It appears that Mrs. Millman has made a tenuous and dependent adjustment since her marriage. She has a history of severe emotional disorder and is at this time showing signs of regression. My diagnostic impression is that of Schizophrenia, Schizoaffective type. In my professional opinion, I feel that it would be detrimental to her mental state if she were separated from her husband at this time. I have recommended to Mrs. Millman that she make arrangements for psychiatric follow-up care in South Carolina."

Two months later, I received a letter from Bella, sent to me c/o Haverford State Hospital, written on Tree of Life Congregation stationary from Columbia, South Carolina. She wrote, "Bobby and I just want to express our thanks for all you did in order to keep him from going to Korea...we have received word that he will be stationed here at Fort Jackson until he gets out of the service. It's a big relief...As you can see, I've changed jobs and now am working at a Jewish Temple not too far from home...I don't plan to join the congregation but at least I've gotten my husband back to going to services which he didn't do before. It has been very helpful for both of us and I'm getting acquainted with the Jewish Religion...Take care of yourself and again, thanks for all your help."

CHAPTER 11:
BELLA AND I START A NEW LIFE

During the year of my analysis, my wife became pregnant with our second child and we took settlement of our first house in Merion Park, Pennsylvania. It was a twenty eight year old stone colonial with mature trees and bushes in a quiet family oriented neighborhood. It had a small back yard and a larger side yard. There was a small enclosed porch on the side facing this side yard, which would become my first private practice office. The house and I were the same age. We enjoyed fixing it up and smiled often. This joyful period soon ended. In May of 1970, my wife went into labor seven weeks early. On a Friday, she went to see her obstetrician. That evening we played bridge with friends. At 1 AM, she started to have contractions. Her due date was not until June 27, 1970. Panicked and scared, I drove her to the Philadelphia College of Osteopathic Medicine Hospital. That Saturday, I did not go for my scheduled therapy session with Dr. Isaac, but stayed at the hospital. That Sunday my Brother-in-law was to be married in New York and my wife was to be in the wedding party.

Later that evening, at 11 PM, on May 9th, my wife delivered a small, perfectly proportioned, fine-looking baby boy. He had my father's dark curly hair. We named him Shawn Franklin after my father, whose Hebrew name was Sraga Fivish. Initially, he did well. Then, he began to have breathing problems and was diagnosed with hyaline membrane disease. I researched and found a neonatologist, Dr. John Boggs at the Pennsylvania Hospital. Our pediatrician refused to allow us to transfer him to the neonatology unit at Pennsylvania Hospital in Philadelphia. His religious beliefs were that what ever happened would be God's will and that we should not interfere. We did not agree but were too young, upset and powerless to fight the authoritarian doctor.

I have no memory of it. However, they tell me that there was only one nurse and myself in the nursery that night that our son stopped breathing. Apparently, I helped give artificial resuscitation. When it was over, I came into my wife's room with tears streaming down my face and told her, "Something terrible has happened." The next day, at my mother's suggestion, we buried Shawn Franklin Zal in a small white casket in my Father's grave. I hoped that my father, whose name Shawn carries, was watching over him. Our son's death affected me for some time but it affected my wife even longer. As well as being her son, Shawn was also part of her body. We knew that we were not alone. The news media had publicized a similar situation when Jackie and Jack Kennedy lost their child, but this did not help our pain.

The doctor advised us to try to become pregnant as soon as possible. Six months later, my wife got pregnant again. The due date was July 28, 1971. She went into labor two months before. However, this time, by keeping herself at complete bed rest, she lasted four weeks longer than she had with Shawn. She delivered in the 36th week of pregnancy. I had promised her anything she wanted if she could hold off delivery until July 1. She asked for a pearl ring. She was determined. On July 1, 1971, our son was born. He was named Fredrick Hirsch Zal after my father, Frank and his maternal great-grandfather Hershel. Fred was also premature and only weighed five pounds. However, he was healthy and thrived. Eight days later, we had a Bris with the immediate family in attendance. My paternal grandmother, in an orange, yellow and white flowered dress with a short orange linen jacket, proudly held the baby. A week and a half later, in Fred's honor on a Sunday, we had a house party for relatives, friends and neighbors. In spite of pain from her c-section, my wife wearing an orange and yellow quilted long dress, her new ring and her hair piled high on her head pushed herself to walk down stairs and participate. Joy was the emotion of the day.

With a new house and a new child, I felt that I had to earn more money. Following my training, I worked part time, 20-30 hours a week, at Haverford State Hospital as a ward psychiatrist, had an office in center city Philadelphia on Monday afternoon and worked overnight at H.S.H. as a house psychiatrist Wednesday evening and sometimes Sunday during the day to make extra money. In my Wednesday evening twelve hours shift, I saw patients in the admission suite and made rounds to write orders for patients mostly for anxiety, sleep problems, heartburn, constipation and occasionally agitation. During the night, I slept in a small resident's room and was on call until the next morning. It would annoy me greatly when a nurse would call me in the middle of the night for a verbal order. My constant complaint was, "Why can't they call me before midnight before I go to sleep?" One night, I asked myself why I was there. The answer was that I wanted and needed the $50.00 a shift that I was being paid. I never complained again.

I also started a private practice in our new home, in Merion Park, in an enclosed porch, barely eight feet by twenty feet in size. It contained two doorways. One was an entranceway leading to the side garden and the other into the living room. We build a partition, which allowed a minuscule waiting room with a radio for soundproofing. In the other section, I was able to have a small desk, a two-drawer file cabinet and a chair for the patient. Although, cramped, it was a beginning. To get started in solo practice, I often had to take low paying and difficult cases that other psychiatrists would turn down. Mental health clinics sent me patients that I saw for medication and therapy for $15.00 for forty-five minutes. This small space was a beehive of emotional conflict. Tired from long hours at work, I would put on my protective garb and try to be helpful. Here, I saw patients whose naked impulses and acting out, accentuated by the closeness of this space, caused me anxiety and concern. Gradually, as I became more professional, I learned to distance myself a little and be objective.

Frieda, a young female artist, who came to me lost in a postpartum depression, was such a patient. At our first interview, Fredda said, "There's a great attraction to die...I keep crying. I can't breath. I feel disconnected, as if this is not happening to me. I don't feel whole." Her biggest complaint was that she could no longer paint. She was afraid that therapy would take her talent away from her. To prevent this from happening, she was very resistant. She used complaints of stomach pains and headaches to cancel sessions. She put up other barriers that slowed the course of therapy. She did many things to avoid looking at me. She would sit on the floor, as a petulant child, with her back toward me. One day, she wore a fancy Mardi gras mask. On another occasion, she wore sunglasses. "You don't want me to see your feelings?" I said. At first, she denied this but gradually, she was able to admit that she was afraid to risk exposing her feelings. "It would be like my body being exposed."

To my chagrin, in that, I was alone in this small office with her without a secretary or other possible witness, Freda tended to sexualize non-sexual situations. Once she came in covering her eyes with a hat commenting, "I'm afraid to get involved with you. I have fantasies about you." I asked her what would happen if we had a sexual or romantic relationship. The answer was that it would interfere with therapy. I also told her that perhaps these thoughts were just resistance to her going forward in treatment.

Freda made continual threats to kill herself. This made me quite nervous. The one redeeming feature that served, as a roadblock to her committing suicide was that she felt guilty thinking of ending it all. "I gave birth to the boy that I wanted. It wouldn't be right to tarnish this gift." She complained about the responsibility of having a child and losing her freedom. "My wings have been clipped." She admitted that she had the baby because she was afraid that her husband would leave. It soon became obvious that Fredda was manipulating the situation. In a joint session with her husband, she cried, cajoled and finally got him to promise that he would get her help for the house so that she would have more time to paint.

Her mood gradually improved, she started painting again and applied for an art grant. She began to sell her paintings. At Christmas, she brought me in two colorful pictures as a present and announced, "I'm doing better. I'm more productive." One painting was entitled: "Happiness of the Pregnant Fish." She called the other one, "Cobwebs of My Mind." They both still hang in my office today. My memory of Fredda is reinforced each time I glance at my wall. I often wonder if she is still painting. I often wonder if she is still alive.

My wife did not like the idea that my daughter could not play in front of the house while I had office hours. My daughter often banged on the door between the office and living room. I was not pleased with my cramped quarters. In spite of these inconveniences, all went well for about two years. One day, a male adolescent schizophrenic went screaming out into the middle of the street and frightened the neighbors. Soon thereafter, I moved my practice to an office building on City Line Avenue in Bala Cynwyd, Pennsylvania. This was my first solo office outside my home. I was excited but anxious that I would be able to pull off this big landmark in my professional life.

During this time, I also rented space on Monday afternoon in downtown Philadelphia in another psychiatrist's office located at the corner of 18th and Chestnut. The richly appointed twelve-story building, with its fancy plaster garland trim of acorns and leaves, and brass, gold, and travertine appointments, matched his personality. Large black wrought iron light fixtures and potted evergreens framed the doorway. The office on the sixth floor was as stylish as the building. Entering into the waiting room, you find two secretaries, typing dictation and sending out bills. I used a plain 8' by 10' room, furnished sparsely with two tan leather Burris chaise lounges and a small table and lamp. In stark contrast, was the doctor's twelve' by fourteen' consultation room, which he had furnished magnificently in a green and gold Grecian motif with an elaborate desk, many ornaments and diplomas, an analyst couch and a beautiful area rug. In those days, the elegant grandeur of this beautiful workplace impressed me. I also learned a lot about the business of psychiatric practice in this office.

I am amazed looking back that I was so impressed at that time. I have realized why. My mother put much value on appearances. She would not allow us to wear blue jeans. She put emphasis on clothing and material things. She actually thought that rich people were nicer people. She told me that my paternal grandfather had owned a department store in Kiev before coming to America. An Aunt later told me that he had actually really sold buttons and ribbons off a peddler's cart.

At the Chestnut Street office, I liked the ability to walk around in town if a patient cancelled. (They often did.). One day, in the spring of 1971, I walked out of the front entrance and found that it was a beautiful bright afternoon. Within 100 feet, I approached Scandia House at 1723 Chestnut Street, which sold Imported Contemporary Furniture. City noises percolated as cars drove by and people rushed to their destinations on the crowded dirty sidewalk. Suddenly, unexpectedly, the thought came into my head that I should walk into Chestnut Street in the path of oncoming traffic. I had never had a suicidal thought before and never had one again. However, there it was. I stood still for several seconds, stunned and frightened. I realized that I was more depressed than I had thought. Up until now, although moody, fatigued at times and often tearful in therapy, I had been functioning normally and doing everything that I had to do. However, my father and Shawn's deaths coupled with my painful analytical experience and the stress of my psychiatric fellowship, starting practice and my Wife's pregnancy all came to a head in that moment. Trained in childhood, by my Father's example, to be a good stoic soldier, I went on. I just continued to walk down Chestnut Street, sad but more aware of my inner strength and vulnerability and forever more empathic with my depressed patients.

During this time, Bob and Bella also continued to walk forward to start their new life. After leaving the Army, in June of 1972, Bob and Bella lived with his maternal grandparents for about a month. They then rented an apartment in Westchester because Bob was attending college there to obtain a masters degree in teaching. He got his degree in June of 1974. That fall, he went back to teach at Penncrest High School. He was not given the same grade or subject matter that he had in 1970. He was unhappy and things did not go well. In the spring, they asked him to resign. He refused. The school went through a legal process, which eventually went to the Pennsylvania Supreme Court. The main sticking point was to determine if Bob was a tenured employee and whether or not the supervisor who had recommended his dismissal had the right to observe him and make such a recommendation, since the supervisor did not have a teaching certificate. The court ruled against Bob and the school dismissed him. He was devastated. His father had recently bought a lunch counter in a farmer's market in southwest Philadelphia. Disillusioned with teaching, Bob went to work for him in the summer of 1975.

In the middle of all this turmoil, Bella announced that she was ready to get pregnant. When they were first married, they had decided not to have children right away. They wanted to wait until they were more settled. Four years had gone by and now Bella said she was ready. She felt that she was getting older (age 29) and wanted to have a baby while she was still young. One night, Bob and Bella were housesitting for a family friend that was on vacation. They decided this was the time. She conceived on the first try. When Bella found out that she was pregnant, she went to tell Bob's family. They hugged her and were excited. However, Bella was embarrassed, got red in the face and ran out of the room. They soon learned that they would have a boy. They worked on a name together and came up with David Edward. The middle name was to honor Bella's brother Will whose full name was William Edward, Jr.

They also decided to move so that they would have more room for a baby. They rented space at the Aronimink Arms Apartment on Township Line Road in Drexel Hill, Pennsylvania. David Edward was born on October 15, 1975. Earlier in the year, Bob's father's business had burnt down and had to be rebuilt. To add to the excitement, the new business opened the week that David was born. They lived at the Aronimink Arms for almost three years. During this time, in order to save money to buy a house, Bob worked as a substitute teacher during the day and continued to work for his father in the evening until 10 or 11 at night. Although Bella complained that he was not home more, he did what he thought he had to do and saw no conflict in his choice to work these long hours.

David was a joy to both Bob and Bella. Her mother however, seemed resentful. Bella and Bob felt that she thrived on tragedy and did not like it when good things happened. When she first saw David, she asked jokingly, "who was Chinese in your family, Bob?" Bella of course did not like this response and was extremely upset. Bob was confused about what to do about having his son circumcised. Bob's family was Jewish and Jewish custom requires a "Bris" or Brit performed by a Mohel (the person who "cuts away" the foreskin in Hebrew.) The word for circumcision in Hebrew is brit, which means "covenant." This refers to a pledge that God made to Abraham (Genesis 17:2), in which He promised to bless Abraham and make him prosper if Abraham, in turn, would be loyal to God. This covenant was entered into and sealed by the act of circumcision. Bob's father and brother gave him the names of several Mohels, but it was finally decided that David should be circumcised in the hospital before he came home. Bob did not know it but biblical law only requires that the son of a Jewish woman has to be circumcised.

There was also the question of how the children would be raised-Catholic or Jewish. Bella had always said that she did not care how the children were brought up. However, if they were to be raised Jewish, Bob would have to take an active role. However, stymied by his lack of religious certainty and his own lack of confidence, Bob could not decide what to do. Bella was forced to take charge and arranged to have David baptized and raised Catholic. Bob later told people, "I was sort of embarrassed but not really. I didn't step up because of my own insecurities about my faith. If I'm not going to step up, she has a right to do it. It is fine."

CHAPTER 12:
OTHER PSYCHIATRIC HOSPITALIZATIONS

After David was born, Bob and Bella talked about buying a house. Bob had been working two jobs since 1975 to save money for this possibility and to have a down payment. It was a race with the clock because interest rates were rising. He had a friend whose father was moving from a row house in Drexel Hill and thought that this house would be perfect for them. Bella did not like it because it did not have a back yard for her to have a garden. She was also worried that if she settled for a row house that she would be there forever. She found a three-bedroom stone and stucco twin (semidetached) house that met all her needs. Bob liked the house but not the neighborhood. He complained that it was in an Irish Catholic area. When he was growing up this section was considered the other side of the tracks. He felt that the Irish have different values and a different perspective on life. Once again, Bella's views prevailed. In July of 1978, David, Bella and Bob moved to their new twin home.

They next decided that they wanted to have a second child. Bella once again felt that she was ready. They both wanted a little girl. Bella soon became pregnant. Somehow, she knew that she would have a girl. Bob seemed more involved this time around and even bought a little dress for the baby in an infant shop across the street from his father's lunch counter business. Much to her amazement, he told Bella, "It was a fun thing to do." Rebecca was born on May 31, 1979. They had picked the name together but tended to call her Becky. This time, both families were happy for them.

Becky was named after Bella's maternal grandmother, who was her favorite and had died in 1978 at age 83. The grandmother was named Rebecca Ancora. Ancora was her maiden name. Bella's full name was Isabelle Ancora. Bob had been told that Ancora was an ancestral name that came from an 18th century Italian immigrant by the name of Peter Ancora, who was somehow related to Bella's mother's side of the family. Her grandmother used to tell Bella that since they named her Ancora that she would get a prize and inherit the family portrait of Peter Ancora.

Their happiness over their new child soon blended into the more mundane realities of their daily life. Bob continued to work long hours and Bella was once again at home alone, now with two young children. David was very active and demanding of Bella's time. She had difficulty coping with his behavior. When Bella complained, Bob did not really understand. He just figured that David was a boy who ran around a lot. To help the situation, Bella often took David to her in-laws' house so that Bob's mother could take care of him. Bella spent any free time that she had planting flowers and rose bushes in her backyard garden.

Left alone in the house with two child, with her husband working long hours, her hormones changing and her mother not available to help, Bella was isolated and under a lot of pressure. To make matters worse, three months after Becky was born, Bella required bladder surgery. She was not prepared for the severity of the surgery and was upset about being away from her baby daughter. When she got home, she was still in pain and doing things by herself. As was her style, she did not ask for help. As in the past, she started not to sleep or eat and became obsessed about religion. She read books on religion, and felt guilty and conflicted about having left the Catholic Church in 1968 and not living the religious life. She continued to function but was clearly upset.

Bob also felt under extreme pressure, His family had just opened a new business and he was working seven days a week. Bob's grandmother told him, "Tell that girl to snap out of it." However, Bob somehow knew that his grandmother did not have a clue about what was going on. Like many, she looked at emotional problems as if they were minor illnesses that the person could control if they wanted to or were stronger. Suddenly, over the course of a few days, Bella's unusual behaviors escalated. She had recurring visions of seeing bottles of aborted babies. Bob felt that they were dreams but Bella felt that it was all real. As in the past, she spoke about the killing of a president and about a conspiracy involving the Kennedys. One night, she called Bob at work and told him that she had ordered a pizza but could not eat it, because someone had put poison on it. On the other end of the phone, Bob took a deep breath and answered, "I don't think so." His fear that Bella would become sick again had come to fruition. He came home from work immediately.

As she regressed into psychosis, Bella again thought of running away to the security of her Grandmother's home in the Pocono Mountains. The day after the pizza incident, she bought a record player and left for the mountains. She said that she wanted to find the priest who had been kind to her in the Mount Pocono Church years before, when she ran away from home and worked at the Buck Hill Hotel. She said that she wanted to serve him. "I want to be with him and take care of him." She felt that this would be the answer to her problems and was looking for penance.

Bob called her Grandparents and they went to the Pocono's and brought her home. Bob knew that she was having a nervous breakdown but did not know what to do. When they got her home, Bob thought of calling me but decided against it. He felt that I had been reluctant to write a letter for him to keep him home from Korea in 1971. Bob thought of Dr. Bruce Hammond and called him for help. He told Bob that he was no longer taking cases and referred them to The Institute of the Pennsylvania Hospital, 111 North Forty Ninth Street, Philadelphia, Pennsylvania.

This period of emotional turmoil brought back memories of Bella's other psychiatric hospitalizations and made it even harder for Bob to decide what to do. Prior to her two admissions to Haverford State Hospital, Bella's Mother had hospitalized her against her will at a psychiatric facility. When she finished high school, she took a job as a mail girl at Smith Kline and French, a pharmaceutical company, on Spring Garden Street in Philadelphia. (This company would eventually become Glaxo Smith Kline.). Her father worked there as a supervisor in the accounting department. In 1966, in the mailroom, she met a boy named Tommy and started to date him regularly. Her father did not approve of the relationship. He would see them sitting outside his house at night in a car and he would become enraged. "God knows what they are doing!" In a fit of over protectiveness, he complained about Tommy at work and got him fired. Bella responded by running away from home and living with Tommy and his mother. A week later, Bella's mother showed up at the door with a doctor that Bella did not know and took her away against her will to Dufur Hospital in Ambler, Pennsylvania. She stayed there involuntarily for 10 days and then they transferred her to Misericordia Hospital where she received twelve electroconvulsive or shock treatments.

Years later, when Bella told Bob about this incident, he was amazed that a nineteen year old girl could be swept way from a house, put into a mental hospital and given shock treatments against her will , because she was rebellious and wouldn't listen to her parents. Unfortunately, in 1966, this was indeed possible. At that time, the Mental Health Act of 1966 was the law. Section 4404 of this Act provided that any authorized person (such as Bella's mother) could submit an application to a treatment facility along with certifications from two physicians and have a person involuntarily committed who **appeared** mentally ill. There was no notice or hearing required. They could keep the person for up to ten days.

After discharge, from Misericordia Hospital, in June of 1966, Bella was furious with her mother and never returned to her parents' house. At first, she lived with her grandmother and grandfather. However, before long, she tried to run away again. In August, she got on a bus to go to her Grandparents' place in the Pocono Mountains but only had enough money to reach Wilkesboro, Pennsylvania and ended up sitting in a diner for a day. One of the waitresses befriended her, took her home with her and subsequently got her a job at the Buck Hill Hotel, a resort in Mount Pocono. Bella worked hard there as a secretary but did not eat very much and lost a lot of weight. Low on funds, she sustained her self on coffee and kitchen leftovers.

For a short period, she dated a fellow employee. He was a bartender but also an alcoholic. She enjoyed riding on his motorcycle and taking trips with him to New Jersey. He of course wanted more physicality than she was willing to give. One night he pushed the issue and she accused him of date rape. She left Buck Hill and found a priest in Mount Pocono who talked to her and calmed her down. Her Grandparents came to get her and took her home to their house. This incident had a great impact on her. A year later, she would have her first admission to Haverford State.

In spite of the ambivalence brought on by these painful memories, Bob finally decided that he had to take Bella to the hospital. They were both impressed by the elegant edifice that was The Institute. She admitted herself voluntarily. Bella was assigned to an attending psychiatrist. He admitted her to a mixed ward with patients of various diagnoses. Bob was very upset. He knew that Bella was psychotic and needed treatment. However, the people that he saw on this ward looked "crazy" to him. At first, he was fearful and reluctant to leave her there. He told the doctor, "these people are nuts. I'm not leaving my wife here." The doctor answered him "What did you expect? These people are mentally ill." Bob felt as if he was leaving her in a dangerous place. However, after some reassurance, he went home. Worried and scared, he wondered if Bella would ever be well again.

Two days later, he got a phone call at 1:30 in the morning. He was told that Bella was leaving the hospital and that he should come and get her or she was going to walk out. When he came to pick her up, Bella told Bob that she had not liked her psychiatrist and that he had made sexual advances to her by putting his hand on her leg and rubbing against her. Part of Bob did not believe that this had really happened. He felt that it was just Bella's perception and not a real act. However, he knew that he could not convince Bella to stay. She often resented it when he tried to be logical and looked at both sides of a story. She wanted him to stick up for her. The doctor gave her a prescription for Haldol, which she took for a brief period. Bob felt that the medication made her like a zombie and was not upset when she would not take it anymore. In a few days, she seemed to be herself and went out in the garden to see her flowers.

CHAPTER 13:
CAREER CHANGES

The 1970's were a time of fashion change. Appearances went 180 degrees from the conservative preppy look of the 1960's. Men grew their hair below the ears. Lapels and ties widened. Ties became canvases sometimes containing pictures of women. Sport shirts had bold designs. Women wore long skirts to go out on Saturday night. Orange and white were popular colors for dresses often with floral patterns.

During this time, I was also moving along quickly in my career. After my fellowship training, I continued to work at Haverford State Hospital. Initially, I was a unit chief on Three South and held the title of Psychiatrist 1. Then, the superintendent, Jack Kremens, M.D., asked me to be the Clinical Director of a new Drug Rehabilitation Unit at the hospital. I knew nothing about the field and was very apprehensive. However I was young, bushy tailed, and flattered that he felt I could do a good job. When I complained that I knew nothing about street drugs, he allowed me to attend a one-week course at the Drug Education and Training Center at Eastern State Psychiatric Institute (EPPI), in conjunction with the Eagleville Hospital and Rehabilitation Center. With certificate in hand, I returned and started to work.

Full of enthusiasm and naiveté, all the staff pushed hard to help this addict population, mostly young men between 18 and 25 years of age, turn their lives around. We ran groups and offered individual psychotherapy. We had family meetings and worked with the vocational rehabilitation department to help get them gain employment. The unit was not popular with the Haverford community. They were afraid and thought that these patients would taint and eventually bring down the neighborhood. After a year and nine months, I was fully burnt out having tried to do administrative and clinical work on the unit. It was just too much for one person. An additional frustration was the fact that I found that the unit had a revolving door. No mater how hard we worked, somehow many of the patients returned to using drugs and we had to readmit them.

Mary Renolyds, R.N., the nurse whom I worked with initially on the third floor, also came to work on the unit. In this tight knit intense group, our friendship grew. From time to time, we had lunch and shared various aspects of our lives. We talked about work and our children. To me Mary seemed like a very liberal, giving and wise individual. She had a knack with people and the patients adored her. Although she was 15 years older than I was, she did not look her age. At that time, I was in my early thirties and I thought that she was about five years older than I was. It was not until years later that I realized our true age difference. Her husband had been a general practitioner who ran his medical practice out of an office in their small single home in Havertown, Pennsylvania, not far from the hospital. It was there that they raised their two daughters. After he passed away suddenly from a heart attack, Mary, then only in her early forties, went back to work at Haverford State Hospital.

I realized that she was going through a transition adjusting to the world as a widow after her husband died. She was dating a black psychiatrist, which was unusual at the time and seemed contrary to what I thought was her conservative personality and background. All I remember is how shocked I was by this revelation. Now, it amazes me how provincial my life view was then. One day I tactfully asked her, "What do you see in Dr. Joe?" She answered, "I've been lonely since my Husband died and he is very kind to me." This interaction started me on the road to liberation from my own racial prejudice. Mary was able to see beyond my professional façade and yet accepted me. Once, I was talking about my interaction with the drug addicts on the unit. She commented, "They trust you. Maybe you have something in common." At the time, I did not understand what she meant. Much later, I realized that she somehow grasped that like the addicts, I too was needy.

I gave many lectures in Delaware County on substance abuse. Although this opportunity helped me grow professionally and hone my skills as a public speaker, I found that people were starting to identify me with drug and alcohol treatment. I learned early on that what a medical specialist puts out in the community is how people see you and determines the types of referrals that you get. I saw myself more as a therapist for general psychiatric patients, and therefore, I gradually tried to distance myself from this substance abuse persona. The clinical director asked me to be the Acting Chief of Male Services in building four. I jumped at the chance. I had my own office on the first floor and my own secretary to type my dictation.

Eight months later, I felt that I needed to make some changes. I had been building my private practice, but I was not ready yet to go off on my own full time. However, I did decide to merge my two private practice sites in Philadelphia and my Merion Park home. I opened an office at the 555 Building on City Line Avenue in Bala Cynwyd, Pennsylvania. I divided the small space on the fourth floor into a waiting room and consultation room. This was my first real office. I was very excited.

I also looked around for other part time employment. In 1974, I took a position as a team leader at a community mental health/mental retardation center in the Roxbourgh section of Philadelphia, Pennsylvania, called Intercommunity Action, Inc. (Interact). Soon I was given the position of Chief of Adult, Adolescent, and Geriatric Services. Interact was housed in an old mansion on Ridge Avenue in a working class section of Philadelphia. It was really a pleasant place to work. It had a large backyard well stocked with Irises and other beautiful flowers. Bella would have loved it. It was the right place to be at this time in history. The psychiatric community was just starting a transition from the state hospital concept of warehousing patients to trying to place more patients in the community.

Although this transition may have been helpful, it also changed the role of the psychiatrist. Interact worked more on the new group or team concept of care, which shattered the hierarchy that had placed the physician at the top. Decisions about patient care were starting to be made in a more democratic way. Doctors, psychologists, social workers and other mental health workers all had an equal say. I felt that the psychiatrist's role was also being diminished in other ways. At times, my signature as a physician became more important than my actual work. Management asked me to run a Prolixin enanthate (fluphenazine) clinic [a long acting antipsychotic medication that, in the mid 1960s, was formulated as an intramuscular injection given once every 2-4 weeks. It became popular for use as a maintenance therapy, particularly for non-compliant patients.] for chronic patients, where I had to give monthly injections and write prescriptions for patients whom I really did not know well. This was the beginning of the mental health managed care model of having a psychologist or social worker see the patient for therapy and having the psychiatrist relegated just to doing medication management. All of this was frustrating and hard for me to adjust to because it conflicted with my older model of training which was based on the premise that it was important to really get to know your patient in order to do effective therapy.

My job at Interact also taught me many things about people in the workplace. Two examples stand out. Once a week, I met with each mental health worker under my supervision. At first, it was astonishing to me that if I missed a session, these professional, adult, competent, psychiatrists, psychologists and social workers were upset. I realized for the first time that they had made me, as the supervisor, into a kind of parent figure and were upset when they did not get their weekly dose of attention. When I finally left this position to go into full time private practice in 1976, the staff wished me well. They threw me a party and even gave me a Cross gold pen on an onyx base which I valued and which still sits on my desk today. However, after this goodbye, they seemed angry with me. I later realized that they were annoyed because they had grown to know me and what I required. A new supervisor would change the playing field and they were afraid of the unknown and angry that they would have to do the work of adjustment.

In the early 1970's, at the urging of Cecil Harris, D.O., I applied for admitting staff privileges at a private psychiatric hospital also in Roxbourgh, then called Fairmount Farm, so that I could start to see private patients who needed hospitalization. Dr. Harris was the first and only D.O. on the staff. Until I became board certified in psychiatry, administration assigned me a staff psychiatrist, an M.D., who had to supervise me and cosign all my orders. Fairmount was located on a large track of land that had been a private farm. It consisted of an administration building and several older small ward buildings. Down the hill was a larger building, with three sections, to house more chronic and regressed patients. These sections were called W, X and Y. Y was a dungeon-like building where patients were taken if they needed confinement or were behaviorally aggressive.

In contrast, there was a new brick building overlooking a grassy knoll filled with beautiful azalea bushes that housed a dining hall where the patients who had ground privileges could eat. It had its own chief. Physicians were treated well. When we were there, we could eat breakfast or lunch free of charge in a physicians dining room. The quarterly staff meetings were also held there. On these evenings, the chef cooked a special dinner including wine for the staff. Fairmount Farm went through a number of transitions. It eventually became the Fairmount Institute and then the Charter Fairmount Institute. Each change made the hospital more focused on the bottom line.

When the ARA took over the beloved dining room and the private chef left, we all felt that it was the end of an era.

After two years at Interact, I made a big decision. I decided to go into private practice full time. A new building had opened down the street from my office at the 555 Building. I negotiated a lease on 600 square feet at Two Bala Plaza. The rent was $425.00 a month. It was a big undertaking complete with architectural plans. The building gave me four walls and a ceiling. I had to pay for the construction to divide the space and put in soundproofing. As was popular in the 1970's, the color scheme was teak, orange and white. It also kept the office bright and cheerful. I was scared and very excited but I was ready to go.

In 1978, I grew a mustache (which looking back was a huge mistake) and took a part time position that I could not turn down. A wealthy entrepreneur from New York who would fly in once a week by helicopter to oversee his new investment purchased Fairmount Farm, now called The Fairmount Institute. Somehow, he learned that I had run a drug treatment unit at Haverford State Hospital. He offered me a good deal of money per hour to be the medical director of a new Alcohol Rehabilitation Unit that he wanted to start. This was in the days before AA affiliation. Once again, I had gotten into a new situation that I had to run without much direction or guidance.

The unit went well. This was the first time that I saw up front the amount of emotional and physical devastation that alcohol could cause a person. It was the first time that I really realized the severity of the depression that some alcoholics suffer after detoxification. Some of this is reactive to their life situation. Some of it, however, is due to the effect of the alcohol itself, which chemically is a depressant. Many had been self-medicating for anxiety and depression but had really just been pouring depression from a bottle into their mouth. It did not take long for me to remember why I had left the Drug Unit at Haverford State Hospital years before. I stuck it out at Fairmount for a year but then went back to full time private practice.

CHAPTER 14:
CONNECTIONS

In the 1980's, Prince Charles and Lady Diana wed and subsequently produced Princes William and Harry. Chicago elected Harold Washington as its first black mayor. Sandra Day O'Conner became the first woman named to the Supreme Court. A disease called AIDS was identified and killed high profile entertainers such as Rock Hudson and Liberace. Ronald Wilson Reagan became the 40th President of the U.S. The Steelers beat the Rams 31-19 in Super Bowel XIV. Kate Smith won the Metal of Freedom for inspiring us with her rendition of "God Bless America." Wars continued, playing out in Afghanistan, Tehran, the Falkland Islands, Lebanon and Beirut. A fan fatally shot Beatle John Lennon.

One of the biggest changes for me during the 1980's was that for the first time, M.D. psychiatric facilities solicited D.O. Psychiatrists. Suddenly D.O. Psychiatric residents and attendings were a hot commodity. They needed our manpower and our patient base. In 1983,

I was even courted by the prestigious Institute of the Pennsylvania Hospital, where Bella had been hospitalized in 1979. However, I turned down this offer, because the Institute, located in West Philadelphia, was really too far from my office to be a convenient hospital for my patient population.

In my entire professional life, only one hospital ever turned down my application for staff privileges. This was the Philadelphia Psychiatric Center (PPC). My application there in 1971 was the first one that they ever received from an Osteopathic Psychiatrist. They told me that although my credentials, both personal and professional, were fine, that there were no guidelines in their by-laws to cover the inclusion of an Osteopathic Physician. I was disappointed and angry both as an individual and as an Osteopathic Psychiatrist.

In 1977, I again became a trailblazer. I reapplied for privileges to PPC. I was initially told that there might still be some "technical points" in their by-lays to bar my application. This surprised me because they had been taking Osteopathic Psychiatric Residents for several years and were now taking Externs from the Philadelphia College of Osteopathic Medicine. Their executive board again turned me down stating that their by-laws required that members of their attending staff have a residency approved by the American Medical Association Council of Education and the American Board of Psychiatry and Neurology. My specialty credentials were through the American College of Neuropsyhciatrists, an Osteopathic Board.

Finally, six years later, a new Medical Director opened his eyes and realized that D.O. psychiatrists could be a good source of new patients for PPC. He sponsored a by-laws change. On February 8,

1984, I received a letter from him indicating: "I understand that your application has been into the Center for quite some time and I have moved to take appropriate action and resolve the problem... (We) hope that you will find this institution an excellent one for the hospitalization and care of your patients."Two months later, I received an official letter telling me that the committee had approved my appointment to the active medical staff as an Attending Psychiatrist. It had taken 13 years, but I had made it through the door. To their credit, I must say, that my colleagues and the staff there were always respectful and inclusive. I was a member of the Utilization Review Committee and subsequently the Medical Executive Committee.

Soon, thereafter, Bella and I reconnected for the first time in thirteen years and she became entangled with the Philadelphia Psychiatric Center. One day in July of 1984, I opened the door of my consultation room in my Bala Cynwyd office and there she was sitting in my waiting room. I was glad to see her but surprised. I had not seen Bella since 1971 when I wrote a letter to Army Community Services, Ft. Jackson, South Carolina on Bob's behalf. I could not imagine how she had found me. I shook her hand warmly and said, "Bella how nice to see you. How did you find me?" She answered, "My Family Physician has offices in this building. I saw your name on the directory. I just stopped by to say hello."

A week later, she called me for an appointment. She explained, "I had a big fight with my mother, last month. We argued over my grandmother's lake property. She tells me one thing and then does what she wants to do. I told her that I never want to see her again and cut off all ties with my parents. The next day I fainted at the pool and had to be taken to the hospital." This was the first time that Bella had taken a firm stand with her mother, rather than just running away. "She also told me that she resented the fact that she had to work, restoring antique furniture, sewing and gardening, to bring money into the house. She admitted that she was angry with Bob. "He's a baby- Peter Pan. We have no security with him working for his father." I told her that I could understand her feelings but wondered if he had any good points. She answered, "He has a sense of humor, is good and kind, is a good lover and patient when I am bitchy." This answer allowed me to assume that although she was upset, the marriage was on solid ground.

The next session focused on health issues and provided a few new bits of personal information. "My health is messed up." She said that she had given up smoking in January, suffered from migraines and was recently diagnosed as having mitral valve prolapse and a racing heart. She seemed quite anxious. She told me that she had had a hysterectomy in 1981 due to endometriosis. She was now having hot flashes and crying spells. "Little things bother me." She had recently been placed on hormone replacement therapy. She continued in a free associative manner and reviewed some of her prior loses. Then out of the blue she announced that she had been sexually abused at age 11 by a neighbor and still felt guilty. She had never told anyone this before. I said, "Bella thank you for sharing this with me. Guilt is a very heavy emotion. I think that you are being much too hard on yourself. You were just a child. It wasn't your fault."

She added, "My mother always made to feel guilty about my sister Rose Marie's problems. She's wacko. She once beat up my grandmother. She now lives on an Indian Reservation in South Dakota with her two children, ages 13 and 18. I found out that she abuses them." At the end of the session, she asked me if I knew a physician by the name of Jim Marks. When I said I did, she got very quiet. I added, "I just know of him professionally. We are not friends." Bella said, "He and Bob wanted me to ask you about the Major Medical payment for your visits. I don't understand what they want you to do. I don't understand the workings of a corrupt mind." This was the first clue that I had that something was going wrong with Bella.

On Friday, August 3rd, she was taken to the emergency room complaining of chest pain. That night, she wrote me a note: "Please accept my apologies for putting you on the spot yesterday...It is comforting to know that you are not Jim's friend...He seems to be involved in all sorts of scams and he's getting my husband involved in them also. Jim happens to be my father-in-law's business partner...the whole place down there is a big front for the mob...I can't understand why my husband likes it down there unless he's getting involved in the corruption also. This is what I was trying to talk with you about yesterday but I thought because you were Jim's friend you went along with everything he did. Sorry! My life is just such a big mess that I often think of packing up my things and moving to Canada. The thought has been in my mind for a long time and one of these days I'm going to take off." This was a second clue.

Her paranoid delusions became more obvious as the days passed. She talked about how Bob had lost his job as a high school teacher in the seventies and went to work with his father. She felt that Jim Marks was associated with the mob. She told Bob, "I don't like it and I'm fearful of them. I don't know what will happen next. A friend of mine works for the State Department in Washington." She also told him, "My big conflict with my mother is over." Bob brought Bella to my office. She was jittery and talked about how people were playing tricks on her and telling lies. "I died on Friday and had to be taken to the Jefferson ER. The atrocities have to stop. Do you believe in reincarnation?" She was overcome with fear that something would happen to her children. Bob told me that she said that she was "ET" and the Queen of Spain. I had Bob take her over to PPC where they admitted her on a voluntary commitment.

I always felt that Bella had come looking for me because she sensed that she was not doing well emotionally and might regress. She had been visiting her family physician in the building for years and must have known I was there. She had never stopped in before.

Her stay at PPC was uneventful. Initially, she had difficulty sleeping, did not eat well and was angry. She denied auditory hallucinations and had questionable visual hallucinations. She described herself as having a psychotic episode. She admitted that the Sunday before admission that she had felt that her sister and brother-in-law were going to kill her mother. Her reality testing improved. She realized that her prior thinking was not true. Our staff Internist cleared her medically. She was maintained on Stelazine 2mg three times a day and Cogentin 2mg daily. She had a therapeutic pass to go out of the hospital for a few hours with Bob. It went well. I discharged her with a diagnosis of Schizophrenia, paranoid type, chronic with acute exacerbation.

As in the past, Bella went to visit her old friend Claire in Virginia to heal. I received a postcard from her dated August 28, 1984 showing a picture of Dark Hollow Falls in Shenandoah National Park. It said, "Hello Dr. Zal, We're in the mountains of Luray. Having a great time.

Today we go to my friend's farm in the middle of nowhere and the kids are looking forward to horseback riding. On Wednesday, we go to Washington, D.C. to visit Ronnie. Ha! Love, Bella."

Chapter 15:
The Stigma of Mental Illness

After her eleven-day hospitalization and her trip to Virginia to recuperate, Bella saw me on an out patient basis weekly. She continued her psychiatric medication. She immediately went back to work as a legal secretary in Media. Her migraines and racing heart did not return. Although, she did not contact her parents, her mother would "pop in" at dinnertime. Bella complained that this would make her angry because it would "catch her off guard." I told her, "Bella your feelings of frustration toward your mother are legitimate. However, you have to consider the source. She means well. It does not pay to tell an unreasonable person like your mother that you are angry. She will most likely only get defensive and throw it all back on you. How else could you have handled this situation? " She thought for a second and then said, "I guess I could have controlled my anger, shared it with Bob and let her do her thing." "Maybe your mother was just trying to keep the door open between you and making an effort to reconnect." "I never thought of it that way."

In therapy, she also talked about her work. At age thirty-seven, Bella remained naive and unworldly in many areas. For instance, she complained about a lesbian who worked in the law office. She said she did not like gay people because, "They know everything; they feel that they are superior; they cling together and shut you out." She talked about another of her favorite topics, religion. She complained about the strictness of the Roman Catholic Religion and said, "I have a little bit of doubt and disappointment." In the middle of November, she requested that she stop therapy until after the holidays because she had so much to do. We agreed that she would get her medications either by calling her family physician or me. She left and I did not see her again for two years.

Bella had always liked plants, flowers, and nature. She and Bob had enjoyed walking through the Morris arboretum in Philadelphia and other beautiful spots while they were dating and when they were first married. She had always been very interested in gardening and had a beautiful garden in the back yard of her home. In 1985, while working in Media as a legal secretary, on a part time basis, she decided to put some flowers outside the office building where she worked. Another lawyer saw her doing it and asked her to put flowers in front of his office building. Thus her gardening business started. Gradually, through word of mouth, she got more customers. Her presentation was unusual. She mixed purple delphinium with yellow daises and red impatiens. Her specialty was roses. Her favorite color was white. They are difficult to grow but she had a special knack. When she started to buy more flowers and supplies at the gardening center, the owner gave her name out to a couple of people and they also became customers. She never had a lot of customers but there was enough to keep her busy. Bob began to help her with the heavier items. He also helped her price jobs and actually worked with her occasionally. The lawyer who was her first customer eventually hired her to work in his office.

In November of 1986, she came back to see me for one session. When I went into the waiting room to welcome her, I saw her sitting with her daughter's head resting on her lap and her son sitting besides her. I thought to myself, "Who seeing this beautiful mother and child portrait could possible suspect that nineteen years ago, when I first met her, she had stood on the third floor landing of building four at Haverford State Hospital agitated and grossly psychotic?" Today, she had a house in the suburbs, a schoolteacher husband with a master's degree, worked regularly and happily tended her garden. Bella introduced me to David and Becky with much pride in her eyes. Her son was eleven and her daughter was seven. She had brought them with her so that I could meet them.

Once alone inside my consultation room, she confided that she had been feeling moody. She had been working full time for the last three or four months "Bob is working seven days a week for his father and as a substitute teacher. He leaves everything up to me. I feel overwhelmed. There has been a breakdown in our communication." I told her that these things happen in a marriage and that she needed to work on the relationship and talk to Bob about what she needed. I have no idea what she did. She left and did not come back to therapy for five years. Interestingly, many years later Bob brought up this period of their life himself without any prompting. He told me, "I remember there was a time that we weren't getting on. She was going to her sister, Mary Kay's house in the mountains near her grandmother's summer home. She (Mary Kay) had kids around

Becky and David's age. I was working all the time in the family business. She really didn't have a life. Our relationship was strained. I felt distant from her; out of touch. At one point, Bella confronted me and told me that she was lonely in spite of all her activity. I realized that things could not stay this way. I wanted things to be better. I decided to look into teaching full time so that I could be home more."

In 1989, Bella and I did meet up again. In that year, Bella decided that she wanted to work for a psychiatrist. One day, I was walking down the hallway toward the elevator that would take me to the patient units at the Philadelphia Psychiatric Center Hospital. I decided to stop in and say hello to one of the physicians whose office was located on my way. I opened the door and to my astonishment, there was Bella sitting behind the desk in his waiting room busily typing away. She smiled and said, "Hello Dr. Zal. I'm Dr. Bush's new secretary." Bella did a good job in this position for eight to ten months. One day Dr. Bush somehow learned of her psychiatric history and immediately had her leave his office and sent her to work as a secretary in another less visible department. Embarrassed and upset, Bella left the hospital soon thereafter.

On October 31, 1989, she wrote me the following letter:

Dear Dr. Zal:

Just a short note to let you know that I have left Philadelphia Psychiatric Center and I am back working for attorneys in Media. I was so crushed by what Dr. Bush did that I had to get into a different environment and it was the best thing I could have done for myself.

The office is a small one, with two attorneys and another secretary and myself. There is no stress and I am closer to home. My friends are here and we meet for lunch every day so I am back in familiar surroundings. Also, my gardening business is in Media so now I can build up that business for next summer. I am working full time for the lawyers and can do my gardening on the weekends for the offices in Media. The one big disadvantage is that I don't have paid medical but its worth more to me knowing that I have my dignity and self-esteem back.

Working for Dr. Bush was a wonderful experience and I feel proud in knowing that I was able to handle the extreme stress and pressure that went with that job. The unfortunate way in which I left however, will be put behind me and the memories of all the wonderful people that I met while I was there will remain with me forever.

The next time that I go to see Dr. Bender, (her family physician), I'll stop by to see you, if your there.

Fondly,
Isabelle

On some level, at the time, I was aware of the stigma that mental health patients face. However, Bella's experience at PPC brought the issue to the forefront of my mind and made me think about it. Even if Bella was over reactive in her analysis of the situation, I felt bad for her having to live in a world where such a thing was possible. I could identify with it being Jewish and an Osteopathic Physician and thus a member of two minorities. I could also relate to it based on my own childhood, where being tall for my age, lack of physical prowess and low self-esteem made me feel isolated and rejected by my peers. Like Bob, I admired Bella's ability to not allow the pain that stigma must have caused her to stop her from moving forward. Now years later, although we have come a long way in the United States in reference to race relations and women's rights, the sigma of mental illness is still a problem. Some of my patients (usually over 50 years old) say, "I hope nobody sees me coming out of your office. They will think that I am crazy."

In May of 1990, a Philadelphia Inquirer columnist interviewed Dr. Bush for an article entitled, "Lying about psychiatric treatment: The pros and cons." The article read as follows:

"If you have undergone psychiatric treatment and you're asked about it – on an application form or in an interview- should you acknowledge it or should you lie?

That was the question I presented to Frank Bush, immediate past president of a mental health organization, whose theme during his year in office was the eradication of the stigma that society tends to place on those with psychiatric problems.

Bush's response: 'Lie.'

His rationale: 'The stigma is there, and to deny it and sacrifice yourself by telling the truth makes no sense...I'm a realist. I have to accept the fact that we have not yet erased stigma. If I advise somebody to tell the truth and they get battered, how can I be their advocate? I'm supposed to protect them from pain, if I can.'"

When Bella read this article, she could not believe it. She ended up writing to the columnist and telling him about her experience. She also sent him flowers.

CHAPTER 16:
CHANGE, RESOLUTION AND GROWTH

As long as I knew her, Bella had always had an ongoing struggle involving her parents, her self-esteem, and her anger. Religion and guilt, however, were the cornerstones of her emotional battle. In 1969, under circumstances that I still did not totally understand, she left the Catholic Church. She initially said that it was caused by her anger at her Mother. I felt that there were missing pieces to the story. It would take many more sessions of therapy before she would feel comfortable telling me the whole truth. In 1990, her friend Claire planned a trip to Europe. Claire wanted to go to England because her brother lived there. She also wanted to visit Holland because her family had come from there. She invited Bella to share this adventure with her.

At the end of September, I received a post card picturing Buckingham Place, London. It read: "Dear Dr. Zal- Having a glorious time in England. The city of London is gorgeous. We went to Canterbury and Rye and did some antique shopping. Lifestyle is much slower here than the states. Takes one back to the 1950's. Isabelle."

On October 28, 1991, Bella visited her family physician, who called me while she was in his office. He told me that she was very nervous and jittery and her appetite was down. He had restarted her on Stelazine. He put her on the phone to make an appointment. "I don't really think it is necessary. I will keep in contact with Dr. Bender's office." She reluctantly accepted an appointment for the next day. When she arrived, she told me the following: "Last night I had a nightmare but I was awake. I felt strange. I felt as if I had died. Thoughts came into my head that were so real that I thought it was all going to happen. I was afraid for my life. I thought my son and my husband would be taken away from me and slaughtered." In spite of all this, she seemed perfectly rational.

As she continued, she started to cry. "I had read about the Holocaust and was moved by what happened to the Jewish people. Last week I read a book on the Kennedy assassination – that's when the decline of the county started." She went on to tell me that she had not worked since April of 1991. "I was with this lawyer a year. He was a lunatic. Bob is working as a teacher and for his father. The kids are fine. David is sixteen and Becky is twelve. There's a lot of friction with my mother." Then suddenly out of the blue she switched gears and stated, "I'm scared. I feel someone will hurt the kids or Bob. Something awful will happen." She finished the session by telling me, "My religion is really frightening. Christ nailed to the cross and all. I started going back to church during the last two weeks."

Concerned that she was regressing again, I suggested a follow-up appointment in the near future. She refused. She promised to keep taking her medication, keep in touch and not watch any violent films or read any books about assassinations. Six days later, she called to tell me that she had gotten a new job, was feeling better and had cut the Stelazine dose down on her own. Five days later, I called her home. I spoke to David who told me, "Mom's on a trip. Dad's at work." He gave me Bob's work number. I called but there was no answer. He called me back two days later. "Isabelle is doing better. She had been taking Vitamin A. She went to Virginia to visit her girlfriend and lowered the Stelazine on her own."

A month later Bella called and made a follow-up appointment. She walked in, sat down and started telling me about the Medjugorje Pilgrimage. She handed me a form that could be used to order a cassette of the Medjugorje Rosary and story and a Yugoslav Airlines brochure about travel to Medjugorje. She explained that Medjugorje is a small parish in Yugoslavia, which traces its history back to 1599. On June 25, 1981, six village children claimed to have sighted the Madonna on the hill behind the village of Bijakovici. Since that time, millions of pilgrims have flocked to this site considering it the holiest of places where the six youths continue to experience visions of the Blessed Virgin. "This place triggered my guilt feelings- all the guilt I have in myself about my mother." I thought that Bella had visited this town while she was in Europe. Years, later, Bob would tell me that she had never gone there. Whether her Medjugorje religious experience was truth or fiction, her thought process after returning from Europe somehow helped Bella start to resolve her issues with the Catholic religion and eventually return to the church.

She went on: "I try to keep peace and not take sides between my sister in South Dakota and my mother. They both call me for support. When she was 15, my sister went to South Dakota to a private school that was connected to a foster home. She visited me for five weeks this past summer. My mother always puts on her very best for me. My sisters see the other side. They know that she harasses the neighbors, drinks until she is unconscious and steals things from our homes. Sometimes I really feel she is Satan."

She then repeated the story, that she had originally told me at Haverford State Hospital, of how, when she was seven, her mother had beaten her with a belt and smashed her head through the window because she and her brother had woken her up from a nap. She also told me how in 9th grade she had fallen and cut her head and her mother would not let her into the house because she was afraid she would get blood on the floor. Then Bella had some insight. "I was so angry about my mother after my sister left that I had started to have tremendous fear. I had paranoid ideas and felt I was dead and not alive." For the first time, she realized that her anger and negative thoughts toward her mother and her memories of childhood were things that could cause her to regress. We talked about anger. "I try to take her with a grain of salt. I have a very dysfunctional family." She ended the session by telling me, "I'm not taking the Stelazine."

The early nineteen nineties were special for me in several ways. I had two books published and became President of the Medical Staff at Belmont Center for Comprehensive Treatment. Since my last year of Fellowship training, I had always written and published educational articles in my field on various topics such as adolescence, depression, geriatrics, etc. I enjoyed writing as a hobby. It also allowed me to research subjects that interested me and further educate myself. For years, I had wanted to actually write a book. In the 1980's, now in my 40's, I decided that it was now or never. In 1980, the American Psychiatric Association's third edition of the Diagnostic and Statistical Manual of Mental Disorders listed panic disorder as a separate diagnostic category, for the first time, under the heading of Anxiety States. This had been previously referred to by the lay public as "high anxiety" Although the new designation was there officially, many professionals were not aware of its ramifications and no specific treatment was yet available.

In 1986, I attended a continuing medical education lecture on Panic Disorder. I was told that there were new drugs in the pharmaceutical company pipelines to treat this entity. It intrigued me and I felt that this topic had potential. I started to research and write on the subject. An article of mine entitled, "Panic Disorder: Is It Emotional or Physical?" appeared in the journal Psychiatric Annals. In 1988, this essay won the Eric W. Martin Memorial Award for outstanding writing given by the American Medical Writers Association. An editor at Human Sciences Press showed interest and offered me a book contract in July of 1988. Very soon thereafter, this company merged with the Plenum Publishing Corporation. Their Insight Books imprint published Panic Disorder: The Great Pretender in 1990. My second book, The Sandwich Generation: Caught Between Growing Children and Aging Parents, followed two years later.

Fueled by my anger over my initial rejections, from PPC (now called Belmont Center for Comprehensive Treatment), many years ago, I made it a point to move up the ladder of the hospital staff. I worked hard on hospital committees and became a Senior Attending. In

1995, they elected me President of their Medical Staff. That had been my goal. I felt as if I should plant a flag on the top of the mountain for the Osteopathic Profession. I was the first D.O. to serve in this position at this institution. They also nominated me for an award given by the Philadelphia Psychiatric Society. At the Benjamin Rush Ball, held at the Philadelphia Country Club, I proudly accepted the Practitioner of the Year Award, for outstanding character, dedication and commitment to patient care. To me this achievement symbolized how much I had grown from that green psychiatric fellow that I was almost thirty years before. I remained active on the Belmont staff until 2002, when I was made Emeritus and stopped hospital practice.

My drive for professional achievement allowed me to grow emotionally and improved my self-esteem. I learned to deal diplomatically with many different types of people and better understand the politics of medicine and hospitals. I felt capable and good about myself. It also allowed me to see my Father in another more human light. I knew that I shared his professional manner. Now, I realized that his philanthropic involvement in various charity organizations probably helped him also grow emotionally. The eleven-year-old boy, that left home to lead his sisters from Russia to America and always took care of everything, had worked hard to maintain a good façade. He had never let me see the child within him.

I had not seen Bella for three years. On October 27, 1994, she again came to see me at the request of her family physician. Now age 47, she had not changed much and still looked younger than her age. She was tense and seemed sad. She had been complaining of nausea for six months. Her physical exam was normal. Her mental status exam was within normal limits. She brought me up to date about her life. "Bob and I haven't been getting along. He gets depressed in the summer time. His father closed the business this year. He got his certificate in elementary education and is working as a teacher full time. Becky is 15 and doing well in school. David is nineteen and a second year film student at Temple University. Bob feels that there is a tension between David and me." She was having migraines once a month around the time that she used to have her period before her hysterectomy. She was still taking Estrogen. She still had her gardening business. She was still bitter and angry about her relationship with her mother and sister. "They tell me that everything is my fault." "You sound pretty frustrated. We have to stop for today. But, why don't you come in again and we can talk more about your family." She would not let me pin her down to a specific follow up appointment. "I'll call you, was all she would say."

Nothing much had changed. Nevertheless, she did seem more relaxed when she left the office. I called her family physician and recommended that if her nausea continued after a trial on the Pepcid that he had prescribed that he should add Xanax (alprazalom) O.25 mg two or three times a day. In December, I received a Christmas card from Bella with a winter scene, a dove and the word Peace on the cover. Inside she had written, "Dear Dr. Zal – Thank you for your care and concern throughout the years and for your gentle way of listening to all my problems. You always make me feel a little nicer about myself. I will call you again soon. Best wishes, Isabelle.

Four and a half months later, I saw Bella again for an office visit. She told me that she had been working for a female attorney two days a week since January. She did billing, typing and used the computer.

She still had her gardening business. Paraphrasing, the title of my second book, she joked, "I'm caught between growing children and an infantile husband. He's either working or lying on the floor watching T.V. Can you believe it, we will be married 24 years in May." She spoke about religion. She commented that she had been married in an Episcopalian Church. She admitted for the first time that she had left the Catholic Church because a priest wanted to date her. She would not elaborate. She said that she had gone back to the Catholic Church in September of 1994. She finished the session by telling me about the kids. "David is still taking film at Temple. Becky has started smoking. I'm worried about her. Would you see her?" We set up a time for the end of the month.

Becky and I spoke three times over the course of four weeks. She was an attractive teenager with long hair, who reminded me of how her mother looked at H.S.H. In our first session, she admitted that she had been feeling depressed for six months. She had had some crying spells and was moody. She did not feel hopeless or helpless. She was easily distracted at times in school. The rest of her mental status examination was normal. She denied any drug or alcohol use. She had started catholic high school in Upper Darby. She found school stressful although she liked art. In December 1994 and January 1995, she had developed Mononucleosis, was out of school for one and a half months and had needed home tutoring. She commented that she did not get along with her counselor. "She puts me down a lot." I asked her to bring some of her artwork to our next session.

On our next session, she brought her sketchbook to show me some of her artwork. I told her that I liked her work. I had her do a House-Tree-Person test where the patient draws a picture incorporating all three of these elements. She drew a small picture of a young girl with medium length hair sitting on a bench by her self on the right side of a house with open curtains on the windows and a tree on the left side. Looking at this drawing, I asked her if she ever felt isolated and alone. She answered that her father was not too interactive with her. We talked about this for a while. I next asked her to draw a male figure on one side of the paper and a female figure on the other side. Her male was a reasonable facsimile of a teenage boy whose shirt showed some detail such as a collar, short sleeves and buttons. She said that he was age 14. The thing she liked the best about him was his shirt. The thing that she liked the least about him was his face.

On the other side, she draw a young girl, larger but very similar in appearance to the girl on the bench. This girl however, had more expressive eyes and seemed to be smiling a little through closed lips. She wore a bracelet on her left wrist. Becky said that this girl was age 13. When I asked her which part she liked best she answered, "Nothing." In response to which part she liked the least, she answered, "The way I drew it; her arms." A general interpretation was that these drawings showed a young woman, who felt younger than her stated age, had low self esteem and felt isolated at times. This did fit the patient. By the next session two weeks later, Becky looked healthier and talked more positively about school and her parents. She again brought her art portfolio and seemed happy when I asked to see her work. I guess the interaction with an accepting encouraging male parent-like figure had helped.

At the end of this visit, Bella was sitting outside in my waiting room. She was delighted to learn that Becky was all right. Although neither of us commented, I think we both knew what was worrying Bella.

It was in her late teens that Bella had started to have emotional problems and she was worried that Becky was following in her footsteps. During these three visits, I could see no evidence that she was heading in that direction. Becky may have looked a little like Bella and shared some aspects of her personality, in that they both had low self-esteem and compensated by trying to do everything right. However, at that time I did not think that Becky carried a genetic predisposition for psychoses.

At the end of May, I received a note from Bella. It said:

Dear Dr. Zal –

Sorry this payment is slow in getting to you. My gardening business has me so busy my head is spinning. Things will slow up after the middle of June but right now I can't see the flowers for the weeds.

Thanks for seeing Becky when she and I needed it the most!

She seems to be doing well and has improved considerably in school.

I'll keep in touch –

Have a great summer!

Isabelle

The next year, I got to spend therapy time with David. At that time, he was a twenty-year-old college student in his junior year at Temple University. He was working 20 hours a week in a video store. I saw him six times between May and August. I opened our first session by explaining the issue of confidentiality. I told him that I would not discuss his case with anyone without his permission. Confidentiality and trust are important variables in doing psychotherapy, particularly with an adolescent patient. I then said, "David, how can I be of some help to you." He answered, "I've been really confused lately. I have a lot of insecurities about relationships. I'm worried about the future. I'm worried about finances." A mental status examination showed that he could be moody but showed no evidence of psychosis or any other serious emotional disorder. He said that he did not drink but had smoked "pot."

He explained that he felt that he was very social but had had no long-term relationships. He admitted that he felt nervous around people. "I feel it is expectations." Half way through the session he blurted out, "I'm attracted more to the same sex." He said that he had dated a girl for one month and was depressed when they broke off. He said that he did not enjoy his first date with a guy. I suggested that perhaps he was experimenting. "No, he answered," I have been aware that I am bisexual for four years." At our second session, it became clear that it was not his sexual orientation that was causing him a problem, but rather his insecurities and anxiety. He set as his goals for therapy: "I want to be more comfortable and secure in relationships. I want to stop worrying. I want to be able to handle more."

I asked him to describe the people that had raised him. He described his mother as being pleasant most of the time. "I get along with her. I always went to her to talk. She is caring, open, affectionate and religious. She gets easily stressed out and yells when she is upset." In reference to his father, he said, "He is not as expressive and not as physical. However, I've always felt his support. I'm concerned about how he feels. He might be disappointed in me. He can yell and be loud when he is angry." He described his mother's family as dysfunctional and not very close. He spoke fondly of and identified with his paternal grandfather. "He's retired. He had a deli but it closed. He's outgoing, personable, and loves life like me. He is strong willed." He mentioned that his father's brother was a drug addict. "I'm worried about him. I want to see him have a good life."

When I asked him what he was looking for in a relationship, he said, "I want to be happy. I want someone who cares about me. I want someone that I can talk to about personal things, about how I feel and be able to share family problems. I care about people and don't get enough back. It's expectations again." We talked about this and tried to give him some perspective. "People are people. They have good and bad points. If you lower your expectations, a little you will not be as disappointed. Then sometimes they might surprise you." In therapy, he also talked about his work at school. He seemed to get positive feedback about his creativity. I asked him about his other interests. He shared that he liked sports, music and followed politics. He had played the cello and been on the track team. After our fourth session, he was going down to the shore with five other Temple Students to a friend's house. "My goal is to meet new people and enjoy myself."

David returned to see me at the end of the summer. He told me that he had met a 19-year-old guy at the end of June, who was a student at the University of Delaware. "I like him because we have open communication. He listens and talks to me like a person. But after the first month I started to worry and feel insecure that I would say the wrong thing." He said that he was suffering from mononucleosis, was tired, had a swollen neck and was experiencing headaches. He also said, "Since June, I feel hostility and distance from Dad. He doesn't communicate. I always went to mom." It soon became clear that he was having trouble telling his parents that he was gay. I volunteered to meet with all three and try to facilitate a discussion. He accepted and said that he would ask his parents.

I met with them the following week. Bella and Bob sat at one end of the large sectional couch that I used for group therapy. David sat at the other end. Bella was quiet and tense but engaged. Bob looked scared like a young boy in the principal's office. I started out talking about how communication can sometimes be difficult in families. I asked David to tell his parents about some of his worries. He told them that he had been nervous and unhappy and wanted to be able to cope better with dating. I tried to ease our way into David's sexual issues by saying that he was also confused about his sexuality. Bella looked calm but Bob stared straight ahead. When the story finally came out, Bella said, "I really don't approve of that but I want him to be happy." (Bella's feelings about the lesbian in the law office flashed through my mind.) Quietly, almost in a whisper, Bob said, "I want him to be happy too."

Later Bob would tell me, "David came to see me and said that we were going to have a meeting with Dr. Zal to discuss something. I didn't know what to think. After the meeting, Bella told me that she had had a good idea about what it would be about. The purpose was for him to tell us that he was gay. I was surprised that she sensed this. I felt like a big dope. I was the smart guy and yet Bella was so much more perceptive of feelings and emotions. She said that she always felt that he was gay and I never did. Looking back, I didn't know what was going on."

David finished his senior year and graduated from Temple University. Then, for two years, he lived at home and worked first for Channel

17 and then for QVC II. He wanted to be in the film business. He had friends from Temple University who lived in Los Angeles. In 1998, after the death of Bella's father, David moved out to the west coast. A few years later, Becky also moved to Los Angeles and took over David's old apartment after he moved to a new place. She had a boy friend in Las Vegas. After a few months, she moved there to be with him. Initially, Bob could not understand Becky's leaving home. Bella on the other hand understood perfectly and patiently told him, "It's because the man she is going to marry lives out there."

Chapter 17:
The Closing

It was not just a collection of buildings and a standard of care that made Haverford State Hospital a special place. The corrective emotional experiences that Bella had there sent her out in the world a stronger person. My time there from 1967 to 1974 helped shape my life. It helped me grow and mature. It increased my self-esteem and confidence and let me start to see my self vocationally as a professional psychiatrist. However, it was the human connections that we formed with people there, their support and nurturing, that were really its greatest gift and most important legacy to both of us. It was there that Bella met the Hammonds and I met Mary Reynolds., RN.

Through the years, Bella kept contact with Drs. Bruce and Anna Hammond. They had been the psychiatrists at Building 12 at Haverford State Hospital, when she was there in 1968. In 1979, Bob called Dr. Bruce for help with Bella, prior to her hospitalization at the Institute of the Pennsylvania Hospital, and found that he had retired. However, they continued to keep in touch. Bruce Hammond was like a father figure to her. They had established a bond of trust. She would call him at times just to talk. As she had with me, she sent them Christmas cards and a note from time to time. In the late nineties, Bella invited the Hammonds to her home for lunch, because she wanted them to see her house and her garden. They came. The Hammonds reciprocated and Bob and Bella joined them for a meal in their Lower Merion home.

Bella shared that she was in the gardening business. The Hammonds asked her to put in some plants around their house. They insisted on paying her something, but Bella refused. Bella's gardening interest also benefited me. My father's one hobby was to work on the lawn and grounds around our house when I was a teenager. I particularly remember him tending to the numerous miniature Phlox perennials, with their various brightly colored fragrant blooms, that bordered one side of the house. This memory of my father working in the sunshine gives me great pleasure. It was one of the few times that I saw my father happy, relaxed and content.

I had looked for this plant for years without success. I asked Bella about phlox. She brought me some pages that looked as if she had ripped them out of a gardening mail order catalogue. They explained and pictured all varieties of this plant. She had written in ink above the section labeled Phlox divaricata, "Is this the phlox your father had?" It was described as a species of dwarf phlox that grew 15 inches tall, has small broad leaves and is covered with clusters of flowers. This seemed to match my memory except I had felt that my father's plants were shorter. Bella also brought me in a bunch of taller white

Phlox, which I planted and enjoyed seeing around my home garden for many years.

Dr. Bruce Hammond had a stroke. Bella continued to visit him occasionally. In January of 2006, he died at age 85. His Wife, now getting forgetful and suffering from mild dementia, still lives alone in their family home in Lower Merion Township, where she and Dr. Bruce had moved in 1950. When I heard of Dr. Bruce Hammond's death one of the thoughts that I had was, "there are not many people left who remember the early days of Haverford State Hospital." It was a unique place that set the standards for inpatient psychiatric care at the time. Through the years, it lost some of its luster but always stood a notch above.

After I left Haverford State, I kept in touch with my friend Mary Reynolds, RN, with whom I had worked initially on Unit 3 North and then on the drug unit. She invited my wife and I to her eldest daughter's wedding. Mary came to our house to visit. She gave us a tree when we moved to a new house in Penn Valley, Pennsylvania. She gave my Daughter a Dalton figurine for her Bas Mitzvah. Our children have fond memories of visiting her in the new house that she bought in Newtown Square, Pennsylvania, which had a pool and a stable for her horse. My son still remembers the turtles that sauntered along a wet ramp from one kiddies' pool to another. As time went by our communication lessened.

I always made it a point to call Mary at Christmas time and visited her occasionally. The last time that I saw her, she was coping with severely diminished sight due to macular degeneration. The wrinkled skin on her face caught me by surprise. She was living in the Newtown Square house with her grandson and eldest daughter, who was now divorced. For a few years, it skipped my mind to call. In December of 2004, something made me pick up the phone. To my sadness, I learned that her youngest daughter had just died in an accident. The next year, I again forgot to call. In December of 2006, around the holidays, I tried to get in touch with her. I could not reach her. Someone had disconnected her phone and I could not find her new number in the phone book or on the internet. I even sent a letter to her old address hoping that the post office would forward it. I heard nothing.

About a month later, one Friday afternoon, I met with a new patient in my Norristown office. As he walked in, he said, "I bring greetings from an old friend of yours, Mary Reynolds. I work with her at Norristown State Hospital." You can imagine my surprise. It turned out that this was really Mary, Jr., Mary's eldest daughter. He told Mary, Jr. that I wanted to talk to her. She called me and gave me her and her mother's cell phone numbers. She told me that she was still living in her mother's house in Newtown Square. However, the sad news was that my friend Mary was now suffering from Alzheimer's disease and had significant memory lapses. We tried to set a date that I could visit with them and perhaps take them both for lunch. It did not happen. Finally, frustrated in my quest, I decided to take a chance and call Mary, Sr. directly.

She answered the phone saying, "How are you dear?" This was her signature salutation to me that had always filled me with such a sense of caring. Hearing her voice took me back thirty-seven years. During the conversation, she was completely lucid. She told me that her daughter, when she went to work, made her stay upstairs and not answer the door. Her mood was good. At the end of our talk, I said, "Thank you for being in my life." She answered instantly, "Thank you for being in mine." We hung up. My eyes watered. She was eighty years old. Somehow, I felt that I would never see her again. I knew that Mary had given me something that my mother never did —positive attention, a gentle kindness and acceptance, which I interpreted as love. For all that and for her friendship, I am eternally grateful to her.

Haverford State Hospital closed after thirty-six years of service on June 30, 1998.

According to the Center for Mental Health Services of the U.S. Public Health Service, in 1962, there were 526,000 people in state and county mental hospitals. In 1996, only 70,000 patients remained institutionalized. This decline was due to new and more effective psychiatric medications, higher health care costs, changing mental health laws, which made it harder to hospitalize someone against their will, and a growing trend toward treating the mentally ill in the community. Haverford's closing was pushed forward by a lawsuit in Pennsylvania filed by mental health advocates on behalf of the H.S.H. patients that used the Americans with Disabilities Act of 1990 to argue that people with mental illness should be kept in the least restrictive setting possible. The U.S. District Court in Philadelphia agreed and set up a timetable for the movement of patient's to community-based care. Philadelphia State Hospital ("Byberry'), located in Northeast Philadelphia, had closed in 1990. Some of Haverford's patients that could not be discharged were transferred to Norristown State Hospital, which remained open.

After its closing, the grounds and buildings remained vacant, abandoned and desolate for many years. Vandalism was common. Its grounds were used for annual Halloween "ghost walks." Just as politics and neighborhood objections stalled its opening for almost ten years, these same factors kept the sale and creation of a redevelopment plan for this beautiful 209-acre property from reaching fruition for eight years until 2006. On December 17, 2002, Haverford Township bought the Haverford State Hospital site, from the State of Pennsylvania for $3.5 million. A year later, the Board of Commissioners, then under Republican control, voted 6-0 to approve an agreement to sell 61 acres of this property for $30.6 million dollars to Haverford Hills Associates L.P., a joint venture of the Goldenberg Group of Blue Bell and Pohlig Builders of Malvern. They were to build 128 age-restricted condominiums, 90 age-restricted carriage houses, 35 one-third acre single-family houses and 45 one-half acre single-family homes. Fourteen acres were left for public recreation and 120 acres for open space. Including roads and storm-water-management systems, this plan would involve 76 acres of the original site.

For the next two years, this plan was attacked and stymied by a public outcry for more recreational and open space, zoning battles, the threat of a possible investigation by the state Attorney General's office and the hiring of a new attorney to oversee renegotiations. After much political upheaval and public outrage, three commissioners lost the November of 2005 election and control of the board shifted to a group of Democrats and independent Republicans. The new land use attorney was able to submit a new proposal, which prioritized conservation. The Haverford Hills group paid the township $500,000 to be used for trails and a nature center, which would belong to the township.

On November 14, 2006, the commissioners voted 7-1 to approve Haverford Reserve, a 55 and older community of 198 condominiums in 6 four-story buildings. There would also be 100 carriage houses that would not be age restricted, but would be designed to appeal to empty nesters. It would be a joint venture of Pohlig Builders and the Goldenberg Group. Haverford Hills Associates, L.P. would pay Haverford Township $17.5 million for a 40 acre building site, which only represented 19% of the 209 acres. Haverford Township would retain ownership of 169.21 acres. They would use 45.51 acres to develop recreational areas. This land would contain four multiuse fields for baseball, soccer and lacrosse, two basketball courts, an amphitheater, picnic areas, hiking and biking trails. 123.7 acres of the land would be dedicated to passive natural woodlands open space.

My wife and I had been talking about downsizing and moving to a fifty-five and older community. We wanted to remain in Montgomery County. We often joked, "Wouldn't it be ironic if we ended up at Haverford Reserve on the grounds of Haverford State Hospital where my career began?"

Chapter 18:
Cancer Therapy

Bella came back into my world on April 3, 2000. I had not seen her for five years. It was a new millennium. In the larger world, we had all worried about the Y2K bug for naught and gave a collective sigh of relief as the New Year started with no computer glitches. The 2000 presidential campaign was underway and Texas Governor George W. Bush and Vice President Al Gore were ahead in the polls and national front-runners for the presidential nomination in their respective parties. The Saint Louis Rams won Super Bowl XXXIV over the Tennessee Titans. The film, "American Beauty" dominated the Oscars taking five awards. Hillary Swank won best actress in a leading role for "Boy's Don't Cry" and Michael Caine won best actor in a supporting role for "The Cider House Rules".

I caught up with Bella's world during the first few minutes of the therapy session. She seemed more subdued. She sat up straight in the chair clutching her purse as she spoke. Becky now age 21 was in college and living with her boyfriend in Las Vegas, Nevada. David was in Los Angeles and had accepted a position as an editing intern for a major film. Bella was working full time in a medical law office. Bob was teaching. "My family is as dysfunctional as ever. My father died in June of 1998, from a blood infection and lymphoma. He was at a nursing home and then they transferred him to Fair Acres (a nine hundred bed facility in Lima, Pennsylvania that was founded as a home for the elderly poor in 1857).Can you believe that my mother still has not buried him?"

"That is hard to believe. It's been almost two years. But why are you surprised?"

She gave me a wry smile and went on to tell me that her older sister, Rose Marie, now living in South Dakota, who was Becky's guardian, had been diagnosed with bowel cancer at age 53 in February of 1999. Bella had flown out in July to see her. Rose Marie died shortly thereafter. When she returned from her visit, Bella had difficulty catching her breath. She saw various doctors and at first, no one could figure it out. "I was sick for six weeks last year. I was having difficulty breathing and I have mitral valve prolapse. I had an MRI of the lung this year at the beginning of March. It showed a nodule with rough edges." I sat on the edge of my chair and leaned forward. Then she hit me with the big news. "A biopsy was positive for cancer. I'm going to have surgery in two days to remove it."

My heart dropped. I had to steady myself to remain calm and focused. I said, "Bella, What unbelievable news. I'm sorry to hear that. How are you dealing with this?"

"I'm angry. I'm tired a lot. I lost 12 pounds. Since my brother was killed in 1968 and my Grandmother died in 1978, I've had to be supportive for all these people (her mother and sisters). I'm concerned about telling my mother. She won't handle it well. Bob and the people at church are being supportive to me."

"It must be a very hard time for you. I'm glad that you have some support."

"I feel upset about the tight schedule. I'm afraid to tell David. He's so sensitive. I have a girlfriend, Claire, in Virginia, who I have known since I was nine. She was my neighbor when we were growing up. She is going to come up after the surgery to take care of me and maybe I will go back with her to Virginia to recuperate."

She came in to see me six weeks later. The surgery the month before had removed the upper lobe of her right lung and some lymph nodes. They also found a spot on her liver. She had lost an additional eight pounds. She had gone from a size eight a few months ago to a size four. She was shrinking. He doctor had scheduled her to start chemotherapy.

"How are you dealing with all this, Bella? It must be very hard."

"I'm frustrated and angry. My sister, Ann, who is bipolar, is causing me stress. My sister, Mary Kay, in Scranton and my girlfriend, Claire, in Virginia are being supportive."

In spite of her distress, she was only mildly depressed. When I questioned her about thoughts of suicide, she denied it. However, she revealed to me, for the first time, that she had tried to commit suicide in 1970. "My brother had been killed and my Grandfather died. A priest had tried to sexually assault me. I took an overdose of pills." Interestingly, she did not mention that Bob had been giving her difficulty at the time about making a commitment. I knew so much about Bella and yet apparently, there were layers and layers yet that I would have to peel back to understand her more fully.

I did not see her again for two months. In July, she reported that an additional spot was found in the right lower lobe of her lung that was not pointed out to her initially. So far, three sessions of chemotherapy had not shrunk the second lesion. "I was really depressed two days ago. This latest twist has thrown me for a loop."

"I can certainly understand. You were hoping for a different outcome and now you feel frustrated, out of control and helpless. Tell me more about how you feel."

"I'm angry with the incompetence of doctors. It's complete negligence. All they had to do is read the piece of paper or look at the film. They also overlooked the liver spot. The cancer is not in my brain or bones…One day in chemotherapy, a technician made a crack about mental illness. I was furious. I told Bob, we're out of here and we left."

"The stigma of mental illness is still alive and well in 2000. How is the family taking this turn of events?"

"David and Becky both came home to see me. It's stressful since the kids came home. I know that they mean well. David is a film editor now. Becky finished one year of college, is working at Vanguard and has a steady boyfriend. This time last year, I went to visit my sister in South Dakota who was dying of cancer. I can't believe we both have the same disease." She looked as if she was going to cry but instead changed the subject. "My mother finally buried my father. It's been two years."

She was maintaining her weight. She was depressed and had occasional crying spells. She was not suicidal and showed no psychotic symptoms. She complained of feeling anxious, fidgety and having headaches. I ordered paroxatine (Paxil), an antidepressant, for her, that I felt would help her mood and her anxiety.

Bella called me at the end of July to tell me that she was going to have surgery on Wednesday, August 2 at the Hospital of the University of Pennsylvania. She told me that she ended up only taking the Paxil one time. She stopped it because she was nauseated from the chemotherapy. I wished her well. I called the hospital on August 8th. She sounded OK and calmly told me that she had a nodule removed that was benign. However, she had suffered a collapse of her lung following surgery.

At Christmas that year, I received a card from Bella. It contained a picture of Bob and Bella walking out of a covered bridge. Bella was carrying their dog, Taffy, a sheltie, a miniature collie. Bob had his arm around Bella and holding her close. They were both smiling and looked like a content couple. On the back of the picture she had written, "As you can see from this picture, there is light at the end of the tunnel! Isabelle. Inside, she wrote, "Dear Dr. Zal – A little note to let you know my treatments are over and I am feeling great. I have been busy since early October in getting the house painted for the holidays. It was a lot of work but it was worth it 'cause it looks wonderful. I have also been very busy making my beeswax candles and selling them at the school where Bob teaches. In short…I'm much too busy to be sick!! (Smiley face) Hope your holidays are happy and healthy for you and your family. Best wishes, Isabelle."

Later, Bob would talk about how happy they were that day and lament how often he had been at work and left Bella to cope with life by herself. His biggest regret was that it had taken him so long to grow up, think about her needs, and truly be an active partner in their marriage. Before, he had felt pushed and pulled between his duty to work and earn a living versus being with Bella and the kids. He felt guilty doing one at the expense of the other. "Although I did not realize it at the time, I was conflicted. People count on you to be there on both sides."

A year went by. In June, Bella came through the door looking fine and announced, "My internist said that I should see you, because stress will kill me not the cancer. She went on to tell me, "Bob is a child in motion. The kitchen caught fire, when Bob left a pot on the stove. It has been a bad year. Becky and David moved out. Bob's father died."

"It must be very hard for you dealing with all these changes. You sound like you feel that you are doing it all alone."

At this point, she became tearful. "I'm angry. I'm surrounded by all this family shit. My youngest sister beat up my mother. People expect me to do everything that I used to do now that the cancer treatments are over."

It's hard being there for everyone, particularly when you want and need support yourself." She looked at me as if to say, "How did you know?"

Her energy was improving and she was sleeping well. Her appetite was poor and she was still experiencing migraine headaches. She was not suicidal or psychotic. We spoke for a while more. By the end of the session, she had calmed down. I ordered another calming antidepressant, Celexa (Citalopram). Then she was gone.

She called me 17 days later, and reported, "The medication didn't work out. I took it twice and it made me sick in my stomach. I'm doing fine otherwise." I told her that I was glad to hear that she was doing better and that she could call me if I could be of help. I also encouraged her to take the medication with food in her stomach and try it again.

Around this time, I made a big decision, which made my life change. After twenty-eight years in Bala Cynwyd, I decided to close this office, when my lease was up in November, see patients two days a week in my home office and share office space with my wife, a family physician, in Norristown, PA. It was here, in Bala Cynwyd, that I had resolved the final piece of the puzzle about my relationship with my father. For the last seven years in this office, I had sublet office space to an older psychiatrist. Conrad Kramer, M.D. was funny and pragmatic. People called him Connie. If you complained that you had to take a detour to get somewhere, he would say, "Did it get you there?" We often talked between patients. If I complained about my parents or family, he would one up me with a story about his life. He told me about his wife who had died and left him with two teenage daughters. He talked about his parents and his early life as an analyst. We spoke about difficult patients. He would make treatment suggestions from his analytic point of view. Over time, I saw him as a mentor, father figure and friend.

Connie had the habit of hitting me hard on the shoulder. Each time, it bothered me. At first, I did not know why. Then, one day, when he hit me, feelings of anger welled up inside of me. I realized that this gesture made me flash back emotionally to the physical punishment that I had received from my father as a child. Submerged feelings had finally come to the surface. When I mentioned this to Connie, he told me that his gesture was a Germanic expression of affection! Closing my office caused him to retire from practice at age 79. On the last day in the office, we shook hands and I gave him a big hug. From time to time, we talk on the phone and still have dinner together.

In August, Bella apparently had been to visit her family physician in the building. I found this note, in her clear handwriting, under my door in my Bala Cynwyd office:

Dear Dr. Zal –

Becky told me you were moving out of your Bala Cynwyd office soon. I stopped by to say "hello" and to drop off the check for Becky's last office visit. Sorry I missed you today. I hope that I will see you again before you leave. Good luck in your new location. Best wishes, Bella.

CHAPTER 19:
FAITH AND HOPE

"The cancer's back," she announced as she came through the door. It was January 3, 2003. I had not seen Bella in one and a half years. However, there she was, as feisty as ever, in her gray slacks with pink double sweater and blond hair. "I started not feeling well in June. By November, they found a lump in my neck. I've had nine radiation treatments and chemotherapy once a week. I'm so angry. I don't like being angry. Before, I was sweet. I haven't had a break. I want to go to the highest mountain and scream, cut me a break."

Before I could say a word, she gave me her other news. "Becky got engaged. They will be getting married in September."

I was stunned and delighted all at the same time. I did not know which announcement to respond to first. The word "congratulations" just fell out of my mouth. "She must be excited."

"Becky is my main worry. She has always been the main focus of my life. She comes to me with all her problems. My best friend, Claire, developed severe headaches during the summer. She went to see her doctor. Her diagnosis was advanced lung cancer. She died in October of 2001. Can you believe it; we both got the same thing?"

"I'm so sorry to hear about Claire. You will miss her. She was a good friend and very supportive to you."

"She left me some money. I used it to buy a piano and a wedding dress. I always wanted a piano. I can play anything by ear."

"I remember your playing the piano at Haverford State. One day you played Ludwig von Beethoven's Fur Elise which I had played on the piano when I was young."

She gave me a subtle smile and said, "Becky is going to wear the dress when she gets married. Coming from Claire will make it even more special."

"Becky will be a beautiful bride. How is David doing?"

"David is in LA. He is working full time as an editor on a TV show, Crime and Punishment."

"I'm angry at the people around me that are unsupportive – my family – my mother and sisters. My older sister, Rosemarie, in South Dakota died in 1999. I was her daughter's guardian. Last year, I brought my niece into my house for six months with her three-year-old child. I thought I was doing a good thing. She just took advantage of us. I am so angry with her. She was $30-40,000.00 in debt. She has nothing to show for it. Maybe she is taking drugs. I feel like an idiot."

Without taking a break, she switched gears. "I never got angry at God before. Many of the things that happened in my life before made me stronger. I credit my faith in God for getting me through. I'm angry with the leaders of the church. In 1969, after my Brother died, a priest took advantage of me and molested me after I told him in confidence that I had been date raped. I dismissed it as an isolated incident. But, I left the church after that for the first time in 23 years."

"Thank you for sharing that with me, Bella. That must have been terrible for you. I often wondered why a woman like you with your sense of spirituality would be conflicted about religion. I remember that you told me part of this story about three years ago. I understand now. You were not angry with God only at the priesthood. After you went to Europe and heard about the pilgrimage to Medjugorje you seemed to put your faith in perspective." Although I tried to be supportive and sympathetic here, I really wondered how many of Bella's sexual revelations –her molestation at age eleven by a neighbor, the incident at Buck Hill, the incident with the psychiatrist at the Institute, and the Priest incident- were reality, fantasy or just sexualized paranoid delusions. We will never know. However, even delusions often have a core of truth. One thing that was true was that guilt festered in Bella over these issues and caused her much pain.

She took a deep breath and stopped for a moment, as if she had emptied her bucket of woe that had built up over the last 18 months. Then unexpectedly, she began to reminisce about Haverford State Hospital. "Do you remember Loretta? She used to dance and squeeze oranges on her head." We both laughed at the memory. "That happened so long ago," I said. "She punched me in the nose and I still have a deviated septum," answered Bella.

I saw Bella eleven times during 2003. Her sessions involved her reporting her progress or lack of progress with her cancer therapy and her sharing her frustrations and feelings of depression. Most of all she shared her plans for Becky's wedding. It was a wonderful distraction from her physical agony. It kept her going. She was determined that she would make it to the wedding. I tried from time to time to say something therapeutic that would give her some insight. I adjusted her antidepressant medication. However, mostly, I just listened and tried to remember what Dr. Varner so wisely had told me thirty-four years ago when I was a Psychiatric Fellow in training. "You don't know what you mean to the patient just being there."

Bella's greatest frustration was that she did not know what was going to happen. She felt helpless. She kept bracing herself for the next step. Her anxiety made her feel that something terrible was going to happen and that she was losing control. She was upset that the doctors did not tell her anything. Initially, she had been told that there was a 25-30% chance that she would live five years. In February, the doctor told her that she had only one year left to live. In March, the doctors told her that they could offer her more aggressive chemotherapy or do nothing. In April, she got a second medical opinion from a new oncologist. A PET scan showed improvement compared to December. The new doctor told her that additional chemotherapy would not benefit her but would only diminish her quality of life. "He told me up front. I feel a lot better. At least I have an opinion for the future." She decided that she would not get any further treatment. She began to realize that there was no cure. Initially, this depressed her. She kept holding on to her faith for strength and hope.

At the end of one of our sessions, she handed me a pure white envelop with an embossed Hallmark emblem on the flap. "I have been collecting Ella Wheeler Wilcox's works for twenty years. Her works all apply to life. I could identify with this particular poem because it's all about the nonsense I've been going through. I wouldn't have been able to get through and survive without my faith." Inside the envelope, on a beautiful folded note of white parchment paper with a gold embossed bee at the top, was typed one of Wilcox's poems of hope written about 1894. It read:

FAITH

I will not doubt, though all my ships at sea
Come drifting home with broken masts and sails;
I shall believe the Hand which never fails,
From seeming evil worketh good for me;
And though I weep because those sails are battered,
Still will I cry, while my best hopes lie shattered,
"I trust in thee."

CHAPTER 20:
BEE'S WAX CANDLES

In therapy, we started to talk about the importance of her quality of life. Bella perked up. Although tired, she began to go out in her garden again and even began looking for a job. "The garden is a mess. Before, I couldn't get motivated." She reported that she felt "pretty good," and even physically stronger. The old Bella was back. "I'm back to bossing everyone around and telling them what to do. I'm having Becky's future in laws over for dinner. I'm a doer. When things need to be done, I'm not happy until they are done." She talked about getting cemetery plots and buying a new rug for the dining room. David visited from California and asked her to come to visit him. She did not feel like going anywhere but told him that she would consider it. She was pleased that he asked.

Her mother came and made an effort to be helpful. She fluffed her pillows, tried to get her to eat and told her to rest more. Bella reacted with irritability and resentment. "I told her off. Why wasn't she there before when I needed her? Now, she comes over unexpectedly and wants to bond. Instead, she pushes my buttons. She made me feel guilty for not going to my sister's wedding. My mother was 21 when I as born, she had a violent temper and had difficulty taking responsibility. My Grandmother took responsibility for me and my sister, Rosemarie. She was always there, very supportive and gave me unconditional love."

"I know. A grandparent can be an important positive force in a person's life. However, Bella perhaps it is time to see that your Mother is limited. You cannot get chocolate milk from a cow that has no milk. But, she does love you in her own way and does the best that she can." She thought about this for a moment but did not say anything.

She countered with a repressed memory that had suddenly come to the fore. "I was in church on Sunday. A woman in the pew behind me was scolding one of her three children who were making noise." The mother said, "I never wanted you anyway" to the middle child. "I began to cry. I remembered the time that we were living with my grandparents in Drexel Hill. My mother had just discovered that she was pregnant with her 5th child. My brother was 5 and I was 7. We were playing around like normal kids. My mother came into the room, grabbed my hair, and smashed my face through the glass window because I woke her up from her nap. Then, she took my brother and beat him up with a belt. She told us how much she hated us. She made us promise that we would never tell anyone. She told my father that I fell over the handle of the vacuum cleaner. It made me feel like I wasn't a good person. I made it a point when I had children that I would never spank them. I would go into the other room until I cooled off."

"Bella, I understand your anger and sense of rejection. However, we cannot pick our parents. How long are you going to be angry, forever?" I could see that she was thinking about this but again, she did not respond. I continued. "Bella, you are a good person in spite of all that." I repeated what I had told her before in therapy, "Bella, you know that you have a right to be angry about those childhood things. Anger is a normal human emotion. It is what you do with it that defines you. When you are angry, you also have to consider the source. You can tell some people that you are annoyed with them and they can take it and work with it constructively. Other people do not do so well with this emotion. They are apt to get defensive, throw it back at you and start an argument. Your mother is not the type of person who you can tell you are angry. You have to share those feelings with Bob, your friends or me."

'I certainly agree! One of the ways that I get rid of anger is to do something humorous as long as it doesn't hurt anybody. One time, my boss made me type a paper for his son. That annoyed me. He used the word human beings over and over again. I typed it as human beans."

Bella's dignity was important to her. "I'm a very private person. I put on a lot of Max Factor makeup so that nobody will know how I feel. Things have changed so much. People used to take pride in their appearance. They wear things out now that I wouldn't wear in my garden. I think how you dress affects how you feel about yourself and how other people feel about you. When I feel really crummy from the chemotherapy, I make it a point to fix my wig and makeup. I get dressed up and it makes me feel good. When I was a teenager, there used to be a Lancôme cream that was so soothing. They phased it out. I don't know why. It was great. I wish I had some now. I get tired physically. I was so sick last week. Poor Bob. He kept making me all kinds of things. They all tasted like I was swallowing shards of broken glass. I'm taking it one day at a time. I'm trying not to lose my identity and just become the cancer patient."

Around this time, a group of fourth graders from St. Charles Elementary school in Drexel Hill, Pennsylvania found out that Bella was ill and wrote her letters of encouragement. After this, they sent her flowers a couple of times. These giving gestures touched her so that she sent each child a bee's wax ornament, in the shape of an angel either holding a lyre or blowing a horn, which she had made. Bella had been making these ornaments and candles for some time. She used to sell them at the flea market and often gave them as gifts.

At the end of June, a repeat CAT scan showed six new cancer nodules in both lungs and around her heart. She brought me a copy of the report. She called her doctor about better pain control.

Her thoughts remained focused on the wedding. At times, she was in a bad mood and tended to worry. "It's the stress of the wedding! I'm giving everyone a hard time about the wedding. I'm the one that's doing all the work. The maid of honor is fusing about her shoes. David is in California and has not been fitted for his tux. I have muscle tension in my neck. I have terrible coughing spells. I should be sitting on the beach eating grapes and chocolate rather than all this frustration. I'm upset with my future son in law. I wanted one song, 'I hope you dance,' by Lee Ann Womack. It's my only request. It's a very nice positive uplifting song. He said it was lame. They have no idea of what it means to have a child and plan a wedding and all your fantasies. He's just a 22-year-old little boy. But I know he loves Becky."

"Weddings can be a stressful time. It's a milestone for the bride and groom as well as their parents. Each brings a separate set of fantasies and expectations to the table."

Becky had a surprise bridal shower in July. Just as Bella had years before, when she went to tell her in-laws that she was pregnant for the first time, Becky, who didn't like surprises, overreacted and didn't handle the high emotion of the moment well. She got upset, complained that she didn't look her best and wanted to run. Her parents took her aside and spoke to her. After this, the day went well.

In August, she and Bob walked into my waiting room carrying two packages wrapped in tissue paper. She presented me with a pair of bee's wax tapered candles, which still sit on the mantel in my house. They have a beautiful sweet smell. In the other package was a six-pointed Jewish star also made of bee's wax. She told me, "Christ is Jewish. People forget that." A piece of gold string attached it to a four-sided tag with sheared edges. On the outside of the tag was a picture of a bee. On the backside were Bella's name, address, and phone number. In side it read, "Star of David." "Our ornaments are made of 100% pure beeswax with a sweet honey fragrance. Buff with cloth to restore luster. Melting point is 142°." When she opened the package one of the points of the star was broken off. She gave poor Bob hell because she felt that he had broken it.

"Everybody is coming to the wedding." She showed me a picture of the three flower girls in their white dresses. "I want to make 400 bee's wax six inch candles and wrap them in white tulle with a name tag so that each couple can have a pair as a take home favor. They got their apartment. I'm too involved with her. I go over there and the apartment is a mess. It makes me crazy. Bob is running around with this Emily Post Book of etiquette. Summer is almost over. I have all these little things to do. Bob and I have all these day trips we want to take."

"I guess that you will have to take time off from the wedding plans and take a mental health day."

In spite of a few mental health days, the tension mounted. On Thursday, August 28, 2003, I got a call from Becky asking for an emergency appointment for Bella. She was agitated, tense and irritable. She was yelling at everyone. I spoke to Bob. The holiday weekend was coming up. I suggested the following week. They wanted her seen sooner. Due to her history of psychosis, I offered to see her later that day although it was my day off.

I saw Bob and Bella together. Bob reported, "It's been extremely stressful. In the past, we rolled with it. Now, Bella isn't rolling anymore."

"I'm pushing," countered Bella. She was nauseated and looked strained. "I've been seeing flashing lights in my eyes since February.

Yesterday for the first time, I woke up and I had a blind spot and it made me feel sick in my stomach." (I wondered about metastases and the need for a brain scan). The cancer spread to my neck in November. They moved the wedding date up. If it hadn't come back, there wouldn't be a wedding now. They keep telling me it will work out. I took on the responsibility of the wedding planner. I'm trying to be helpful. I'm not getting any cooperation. I feel that I'm being taken for granted. One of the bridesmaids broke down in tears at the dressmakers'. Let's give Mom something to do so that she doesn't think a lot. I may just leave the reception and go see my thorn aster (beekeeper) to relax. I'm not allowed to use the word lame. Maybe I should say deformed, disabled or broken. They're so negative. Bob can't say anything. I quit. I'm physically tired. I'm coughing and tired." It was obvious to me that Bella was worried about making it to the wedding.

As Bella ranted, Bob became tearful. At the end of the session, he handed me a note. "I want to discuss something but not in front of Bella." The note said, "Bella for the first time told me that she had always wanted that Carly Simon song ('you are the love of my life') for her and David to dance to at his wedding. It broke my heart. She said that she doesn't begrudge David, (for being gay)." Later, he explained that he felt sad because he realized that Bella would never live to see David settled down or with a life partner and that, she would never dance at his wedding.

On September 10, 2003, Bella was smiling and her mood was better. "I've been taking my medicine and feeling more relaxed. Things have quieted down." Mentally, I feel better. I'm putting the remaining wedding tasks on the bride and groom and Bob just like you suggested. It takes the stress off of me." However, physically, she was not doing as well. Her coughing spells had increased and she had restarted chemotherapy once a week.

She brought me a set of the candles, wrapped in a white bow that she would give out to each couple at the wedding. They were beautiful. "I have to make 72 more bee's wax candles and I only have 12 molds." She reminded me what the candles represented. "My grandmother lit candles when we came over to eat. At 4 PM, she got bathed and dressed. Then she prepared dinner. She lit the candles and it set the mood for the dinner every night. I felt safe and all was right with the world. I liked being over there. I miss them. My mother didn't inherit any of my grandmother's virtues." Her eyes filled up as she continued. "I wish that my grandparents could be at Becky's wedding."

I did not see Bella again until after the wedding. On November 17, 2003, she walked into my office neatly dressed in a gray sweater with pink and mauve flowers, a pink mock turtleneck sweater and heather gray pants. She wore pearl earrings and a pearl pin on the left side of her necklace. "I'm hanging in there. I was depressed when I called. They started me on a new chemotherapy pill. It cost $2000 for 30 pills. It was supposed to decrease the coughing and the pain. Instead, it made me feel nauseated, decreased my appetite, gave me acne and made me tired. Saturday, the pain was so bad that I had to take a Dilaudid (hydromorphone HCL). He didn't tell me my eye lashes would fall out! I can do simple things around the house. But, just thinking about the holidays gets me tired."

"I feel hopeless. I wish I could do more. I see beautiful outfits. I wish I could work again so that I could get all dressed up. I would like to work but I know I can't handle it. I feel helpless, only when people try to do too much for me. They mean well. They want to drive me everywhere."

"Maybe they just want to spend time with you."
She thought for a minute and then said, "I never thought about it like that before."

"I've been sick so long. It's been wearing on the family. I'm not easy to live with. I worry about Bob. If anything happens to me, he will be a lost puppy. Who will take care of him? He is making great strides getting Taffy, the dog, to like him. I encourage him to be more involved with his sisters. I would like to see him met another woman (after I am gone) and settle down."

Some time later, Bob told me, "Bella was jealous of my family because she felt that the time I shared with them took away from her. My family, although caring, were consuming. You could not get away. There was nothing separate. I realize now that there was a time when we were younger that Bella needed my attention. It was unfair of me to have given my family so much of my time. We needed time together. By the time, I realized this, it was too late and Bella was ill. I always felt that she was totally dependent on me." It is funny that both Bob and Bella saw each other as a child that needed to be cared for. Perhaps, at different times and under different circumstances, they were both right. They could both see the child inside the adult that they loved.

"The wedding was wonderful. Fall is my favorite time of the year. It's cool with decreased humidity. My energy level is better. I never did well in the summer. Even as a kid, I always had a headache and was sick to my stomach in the summer. We are going to go on vacation and visit David. I spent so much time the last year with Becky. We never went away before because of the dog." I encouraged her to continue spending quality time on day trips just with Bob.

She ended the session by taking a small album containing some wedding pictures out of her bag. There was Bella in a long pale blue gown with matching jacket looking elegant on the arm of Bob, slightly off balance, wearing a white tuxedo jacket with black vest and bow tie and a white rose buttoner. Becky, looking Grace Kelly beautiful, was wearing a white wedding dress with a satin bottom and a deep sweetheart neckline brocaded top covered with delicate lace and small pearls, which Bella had paid for with her inheritance money from her friend Claire. She carried a large bouquet of white roses, small white orchids, green ferns and hanging ivy. David was handsome in his black tuxedo. I held back tears as I commented on the pictures. Bella and all 400 of her bee's wax candles had made it to Becky's wedding.

Chapter 21:
The Final Days

I last saw Bella on April 5, 2004. I had not seen her since the middle of November. I was a little anxious and uptight waiting for her to arrive. I did not know what to expect or how she would be. She walked in as usual, neatly dressed and trying to smile. She wore a light coat and a long embroidered scarf. Under this, she wore a sweater, turtleneck and skirt. As was often her style, she was all in pink and gray. Everything matched. She carried a box of tissues. She was very thin. She had weighed 107 lbs in September and weighed 94 pounds now. Her blond hair had started to fall out and she had cut it short. For the first time, I could see the protruding ears that had bothered her Mother. She related that she had not been feeling well since Christmas. She had switched to a new oncologist and had had chemotherapy, which made her feel nauseated.

One night, in March, Bob had taken her to the Lankenau hospital Emergency Room, due to dehydration and vomiting. They admitted her. Tests showed that the cancer had metastasized to her brain. The doctors suggested radiation to the brain. They told her that she had 3-6 months to live if she did not agree and 1-2 years if she had the treatment. She agreed. Both she and Bob felt that "time is important." She had 14 consecutive days of radiation to the brain. The treatments had finished one week earlier.

Bob had called me eight days earlier to make an appointment for Bella. The Sunday before our appointment, he called again. "Doctor Zal, I don't know what to do. Help me." He related that Bella was disoriented, mildly confused, and even aggressive at times. The night before, he had walked into the bathroom to find her naked trying to put cream all over her body. She said, "Help me put the cream on. I want to put the cream on my wrinkles but I don't know how. I want to be beautiful. I want to radiate my feet." Recently, her doctor had placed Bella on steroids. Bob did not know if the reaction was due to the steroids or the radiation. (I wondered about the cancer metastasis to the brain.) He told me that the oncology resident on call that weekend wanted to prescribe Haldol and that he was concerned. I called the oncology resident and told her about Bella's earlier good response to Stelazine. She had never heard of this older medication but agreed to give it a trial. She told Bob to give Bella 5 mg of Stelazine that night and start her on one tablet twice a day on Monday. She continued to be irritable. Bob called me Monday. He said that Bella seemed angrier. He wanted to know if he could increase the Stelazine. That morning, she had sprayed air freshener into her mouth because she felt that her mouth smelled.

In the office the next day, I did a mental status examination.

"Bella, I have to ask you a few questions to see how you are doing," I said. "There are no trick questions. Just answer them the best you can."

"What month and year is it now?"

"It is October of 1993

"Where are you now?"

"I'm in Dr. Zal's office of course."

"How has your mood been since I last saw you in November? Have you been feeling depressed, sad or blue?"

"I haven't been feeling depressed," she answered, "but I have felt blue and sad for a few months."

"How is your energy? Are you still doing the things that you like to do?"

She said, "I'm tired. I'm not doing my best. I haven't been out in the garden picking flowers or gardening. I haven't been doing things that I like to do."

"Bella, do you wish you were dead?"

"No!"

"Do you want to harm yourself?"

She looked annoyed at my question and responded, "I wouldn't kill myself. I have too much to do. My family needs me. God wouldn't approve."

She sounded wound-up. I asked her if she felt anxious.

She responded, "I feel very nervous and tense. The TV and computer annoy me. I don't know why they're on. I'm ready to get away for a little bit to someplace pretty, someplace beautiful."

"What stops you from relaxing more?" I asked.

"I have to try and finish everything that I promised I would do for Bob and the house. I went on a buying spurt. I made phone calls. I want to have the rug cleaned and bring it from the dining room to the living room. I want to get gas fireplace logs. I want to get a teapot. I feel I'm very special to my Husband and Daughter. God has no special people. I wish he had. I'm right here where I'm supposed to be doing what I'm supposed to be doing." This rapid, pressured, speech sounded almost hypomanic to me. I wondered about racing thoughts.

"Bella, you seem very stressed and upset. What is bothering you?"

She answered in the same-pressured way, "My hair bothers me. I can only do so much for myself. People have to help me. My mother bothers me. She cares about me in her own goofy way. She's goofy as goofy can be. I'm worried about Taffy, our dog. She's a neurotic dog that should be on doggy Prozac. She's a one-person dog. She will only go to me and not Bob. What will Bob do when I'm gone?"

In spite of her medical situation, Bella remained positive and upbeat. She ended the session by saying, "Bob is wonderful to me. He's always been wonderful. I think I'm doing better than they anticipated. I'm doing OK. I probably will be a little better." I smiled and said a silent prayer. I gave her a prescription for medication, some instructions and a modicum of hope and walked her out to the waiting room. There Bob was sitting looking fatigued and drained. We exchanged pleasantries. Bella turned, waved and smiled as they went out the door. Then she was gone.

Later Bob told me, "It seemed to happen so quickly. The last few weeks, I realized that I really needed to be there and I took off from school. We still had been doing stuff. We went out in the car. I had been carrying her up the stairs at night but she could walk down herself. We're doing everything we always did and then suddenly in the third week of April, hospice is there and she is dying. There is a hospital bed, an oxygen mask and a special kit with liquid morphine. The last four years, we had been waiting for the other shoe to drop and now it was happening. I couldn't believe it. She seemed to be doing better. I was surprised that it was happening."

Bob and Bella's thirty-third anniversary was May 8, 2004. They were limited in what they could do to celebrate. People from Bob's school had sent in some food. They had dinner at home, but Bella's appetite was limited. Afterwards, they looked through an anniversary album that Becky had made and given to them as a gift. They reminisced about the weekend at the Brandywine Hotel, a bed and breakfast that the kids had given them as a Christmas present the year before. Bella had not been well enough to go at the time, but they talked about using it in the future.

One night, the following week, one of the teachers from Bob's school visited. He had been one of Becky's teachers in seventh grade. They joked about a science assignment that he had given her that had made them all crazy. As youngsters do, Becky had left the project, which was to make a car propelled by a rubber band or some other external apparatus, go until the last minute. Bob came home from work at his Father's lunch counter at 11 o'clock at night and they all ran around to get parts for the car. As is often the case, they all got upset and stressed. Bella swore that she had had enough of public school and threatened to switch Becky to parochial school.

"The last twenty four hours, she had trouble breathing. She didn't want to take the morphine but she did. That night, I carried Bella upstairs as usual. She slept off and on and I sat on the side of the bed all night. In the morning, Becky left to pick up David who was due to arrive on a 10AM flight from California. We were alone. Bella seemed to pass out and then her eyes got real big and she called for her mommy in a child's voice. It was sort of scary. The hardest thing was that I felt it wasn't fair. Her life had been so hard and it was amazing what she had accomplished. Nobody ever cut her a break. I though about everything you do with a partner, how long it takes to really love someone and how we really became a couple. Just when we finally realized that we really cared about each other, she got sick. I knew I really loved her and she really loved me."

Bella died at 8 AM on May 15, 2004. She was 57 years old. I know that she went to some place beautiful.

Bob called me at 5 PM that day. I was in Hot Springs, Virginia giving a lecture. My cell phone did not get reception in the mountains. The next day, at 4 PM, when I retrieved Bob's message, I called him back but there was no answer. I reached his home at 8:30 PM. Becky answered the phone and told me that her mother had died on Thursday. Like her family, I had been mourning her loss during her long illness and expected the news. However, the actuality still shook me. Before I could respond, Becky said, "I'm glad she died so she won't be in severe pain. David was due to come in on Thursday but got there after mother died. She will have a Christian burial on Tuesday, May 18, 2004. There will be a 10 AM mass followed by a burial in Media, at my mother and father's gravesite. This will be followed by a luncheon." Becky was so much like her mother. When she was under stress, she took care of business.

Bob got on the phone. I said, "My condolences. She was a special lady. I will miss her." I could sense him tearing up on the other end of the phone. I also felt tears come to my eyes. "Thank you", he said, "she had some good days with her mom at the end. Bella finally understood (that her mother was what she was). Her mother didn't get it. She was glad just to be needed. Bella thought the world of you. I appreciate your support through the years. It's ironic. Bella met you 37 years ago. It's been a source of security for all of us. There were two very stable people in her life – Dr. Bruce Hammond and you."

"Thank you. She will be missed."

At that moment, I also thought about how much time had passed, how much had happened in both our lives and how much we had grown since we first met at Haverford State Hospital. Now that Bella and Mary Reynolds were dead and H.S.H. was soon to be demolished, my ties to that period of my life were gone.

Bella never knew that I felt that we were kindred spirits. As her therapist, there was much personal information that I could not share with her. To her, we were patient and physician/ therapist. However,

I knew that, in some ways, we were also two people who were on the same wavelength. We had shared some of the same emotional life experiences. In a way, we had grown up together. This feeling of harmony as well as our long history together created a special rapport, helped her trust me, and allowed me to be more empathic. It did not require words or explanation. It was just something that we both felt.

I got off the phone and told my wife, "Bella passed away." Although, she could see that I looked distraught, my reaction initially confused her. She knew that I was seeing a former patient, from Haverford State Hospital, for therapy, who had lung cancer, but she did not know her name. She knew her only as 'the Bee's Wax lady,' because of the handmade gifts that Bella had given me.

I sent white roses with baby's breath. The card read, "My Condolences - Bella touched all of our lives in a special way."

The children from the St. Charles Elementary School in Drexel Hill, who had written her letters of encouragement and sent her flowers in 2003, asked permission and attended her mass. The Choir from the Drexel Hill Middle School, who had serenaded Bob and Bella at Christmas in their home, as they did each year for people who were ill, sang at the funeral.

A month later, I received a plain white thank you card from Bob with a standard saying printed inside. On the flap, he had written – "Dear Dr. Zal, Thank you for the beautiful flowers you sent. More importantly thank you for having faith in Bella and being her friend

and trusted doctor for many years. Sincerely, Bob, David and Becky."
I was truly touched.

Bella was not only special to her family. She was also special to me.
I will miss her dry humor, her intense opinions, her take-charge
attitude and her sense of assuredness. She added something to my
life. She was my friend. When I first met her at Haverford State
Hospital, she reminded me of Medusa. The beheading of Medusa
symbolizes the ultimate silencing of female wisdom and expression.
It is an act that stops her growth and limits her potential. Her spirit,
her mind and her spiritual powers are killed. Bella's psychosis could
very well have beheaded her. Instead, in spite of a history of severe
mental illness and a dysfunctional family background, she was a
survivor and did the very best with what she had. She married, had
children, worked, ran a business, had friends and tended her garden.
In the end, it was not mental illness that ravished her, but rather
physical disease.

I will always remember Bella's wonderful spirit, feisty personality
and determination. Although we lived in two parallel worlds, had
different genetics and followed different paths, I could identify with
many of her feelings and experiences. I could empathize with her
life struggles as well as her joys. Many times during the years that
we spent together, I said to myself, "There but for the grace of God
go I." In my father's day, if a gentleman passed a woman whom he
knew on the street, he would tip his hat. It was a gesture of respect,
admiration and much more. So, as my father would say, "Bella, I tip
my hat to you."

EPILOGUE
MY LIFE IN PSYCHIATRY

"You've had a wonderful career," my colleagues say, much to my chagrin. "What do you mean, <u>had</u>," I respond. "After thirty-eight years, as a psychiatrist, I am still working, learning and growing every day." The seasoned physician, like the experienced lover, has much to offer, due to a more mature understanding of himself or herself and others. Psychiatry is an art involving patience, tolerance, trust, integrity, empathy, insight and the ability to listen carefully to another person. It is also a science involving an ever-changing panorama of information, which one must learn, integrate and cope with. This is why the psychiatric life is always a work in progress.

In each decade of my psychiatric career, there have been sweeping advances and new understanding in the field of psychopharmacology. There have been changes in diagnostic nomenclature to learn and new mental health laws to understand. In 1973, President Richard Nixon signed the Health Maintenance Organization Act. At that time, I did not realize that the gradual encroachment of managed care would become one of the most aggravating changes in medicine, would limit my ability to give patient care and erode the role of the psychiatrist. Many HMO plans limit the patient's psychiatric outpatient visits to 20 per year. Many insurance plans require prior authorization for certain medications and hand out mental health visits in small amounts, requiring physicians to fill out forms to obtain additional visits. The psychiatrist now is often marginalized and asked to do only medication management. This split limits the physician's control over the therapeutic process and interferes with the patient-physician relationship.

I have been privileged to view the field of psychiatry from several vantage points. I was a fellow in psychiatry, a medical director at a drug rehabilitation unit, chief of adult and adolescent services at a local mental health clinic and the medical director at an alcohol rehabilitation unit. I have also been in the private practice of psychiatry since 1970 doing individual psychotherapy, medication management, group and couples therapy. For the majority of my solo practice career, I have worked without office assistance and served as chief cook and bottle washer doing scheduling, billing and often my own typing. I have sat on many professional committees, done utilization review and served as president of the medical staff of a large private psychiatric hospital.

Psychopharmacology

The shift in psychiatric treatment really started in 1952, when major tranquilizers were introduced, with the discovery of chlorpromazine (Thorazine), and greatly influenced the treatment of psychosis.

These antipsychotic agents, the phenothiazines, such as Mellaril (thioridazine), Trilafon (perphenazine) and Stelazine (trifluoperazine), helped me treat Bella, Lorraine and John at Haverford State Hospital. As time went by, psychoactive drugs continued to become a reality and further shifted the focus of treatment from an analytic Freudian model to an emphasis on the physiologic mechanisms and brain chemistry involved in mental illness. In the mid-1960s, lithium was found to treat manic-depressive illness. Looking back, I wonder if U.S. psychiatrist's tendency, at the time, to diagnoses many more psychotic people with the label of schizophrenia rather than manic depressive disorder (later called bipolar disorder) was not due to a lack of clear cut treatment for bipolar disorder until 1965. In Europe, psychiatrists had tended to make a diagnosis of manic-depressive disorder much more frequently. Today there are even those who suggest, based on genetic data that patients diagnosed with schizophrenia really suffer from bipolar disorder with psychotic features. In any case, the diagnosis of Bipolar disorder is made much more often in the United States today.

This may certainly have been true in Bella's case. Looking back, she did represent a diagnostic dilemma. On the one side, she had symptoms of grandiosity, religiosity, and delusional often-paranoid ideation, which clearly put her in the Schizophrenic camp. However, there was also the issue that she always bought something expensive when she started to regress and showed reckless running away behavior. At those times, she had a decreased need for sleep. This could have been hypomania. These periods were always preceded by significant changes in appetite and sleep patterns and feelings of guilt and anger, which could be construed as depression. There is also the issue that she tended to reconstitute quickly and functioned very well when she was not psychotic. Years later, I learned that she had a sister, Ann, who had been diagnosed as being Bipolar. This would make you suspect a family history with a genetic predisposition. Perhaps, Bella was really a Bipolar II disorder with psychotic features and not schizophrenic as we thought at the time.

The increase in compounds to treat mental illness after this caused Time magazine in the early 1970s to proclaim on one of its covers that the twentieth century was the era of psychopharmacology. The 1980s brought with it new research information in psychopharmacology, particularly in the area of anxiety and panic disorder. In 1988, Prozac (fluoxetine), the first of a new class of antidepressants, the selective serotonin reuptake inhibitors (SSRIs), was introduced. These compounds would improve the side effect profile compared to the older Tricyclic Antidepressants. One by one, the SSRIs have received FDA approval for the treatment of each of the anxiety disorders. Suddenly, there was something we could offer to help, not only panic disorder, but also obsessive-compulsive disorder, posttraumatic stress disorder and social phobias. This century has brought us atypical antipsychotic medications, which have improved side effect profiles, given us more efficacious treatment options and moved us further into the age of the brain. It has been quite a ride.

Change in Mental Health Laws

When I started my training at Haverford State Hospital in 1967, a person could be hospitalized in Pennsylvania against their will, with very little provocation, because they appeared to need emotional help. This is what happened to Bella during her initial involuntary hospitalizations at Dufur, Misericordia and Haverford

State Hospitals. The Mental Health and Retardation Act of 1966 (P.L.6, 50 Pa.C.S. 4101, et seq.), under Section 4404, allowed an authorized person, such as a relative (like Bella's mother), to submit an application to a treatment facility, in the interest of someone who appeared mentally ill. The application had to be accompanied by certificates of two physicians who had examined the person within one week and within 30 days of the admission. No notice or hearing was required. The person could remain committed involuntarily for as long as the Court ordered or until the facility determined that treatment was no longer needed.

Ten years later, in 1976, the Mental Health Procedures Act (P.L. 817) repealed the 1966 Act, except insofar as it related to mental retardation, setting up more significant safeguards for the individual. Under section 302 of this new act, a person could be involuntarily committed for 120 hours either by certification of a physician, as to the need for examination, a warrant issued by the county administrator authorizing examination or application by a physician or other authorized person who had personally observed conduct showing the need for such examination. Once at the facility, the person had to be informed of the reasons for emergency examination and of the right to communicate immediately with others. The commitment was limited to 120 hours unless the person signed a voluntary commitment or the facility applied to the court for a 20-day extension under section 303.

Court ordered involuntary commitments could be further extended for an additional 90 days, under section 304, for severely mentally ill persons who presented a clear and present danger to themselves and others. This could only happen at the request of the county administrator or the director of the treatment facility. The patient had to be notified and a hearing had to be held before this extended treatment could be ordered. Under section 305, an additional 180 days of involuntary treatment could be court ordered where appropriate if the same procedure was followed.

Stigma in Mental Health

In spite of advances in other areas, many are still unable to recognize that mental illness is a real disease that is as common and treatable as physical illness. Many still see mental illness as a mark of disgrace. Because of this, some patients still prefer to pay cash rather than use their insurance. Some will not tell their family and friends that they are going for treatment. Some ask me not to call them at their place of employment. Underneath their symptoms, the mentally ill are real people with the same feelings as you and I. When well, they can perform up to their potential and be quite "normal".

Stigma creates many added problems for them to overcome. People who remember being picked on as a youngster for being too short or too tall, too fat or too thin, or being excluded from a clique as an adolescent, can understand the corrosive effect that stigma can have on the mentally ill. It can create feelings of embarrassment and humiliation, lower their self-esteem and intensify feelings of inadequacy. It can cause family and friends to turn their backs on them and create barriers to their seeking and receiving help. Many believe incorrectly, like Bob's grandmother, that an individual with a mental disorder is weak and should just "snap out of it" or that they are all potentially dangerous. Once a person is labeled with a history of mental illness, many are denied housing, insurance and employment.

Insurance companies have discriminated against mental health patients putting an unfair financial burden on mental health patients and their families. When I first started practice, in 1970, Medicare limited the number of psychiatric out patient visits to two sessions a year. Congress passed the first federal mental health parity law in 1996. It mandated parity coverage between mental and physical disorders in lifetime and annual dollar limits. However, Medicare still only paid 50% for out patient mental health care. Although we have come a long way, Managed Care Companies still limit the number of mental health visits a patient could receive per year and some nursing homes deny admission to patients with psychiatric symptoms. It was not until recently, with the passage of the Paul Wellstone and Pete Domenici Mental Health Parity and Addiction Equity Act of 2008, that mental health coverage has moved forward. Although the bill went into effect in 2009, it will be phased in gradually. For instance, in reference to reimbursement, Medicare will increase their outpatient mental health benefits rate to 55% in 2010 & 2011. Finally, in 2014, it will be the full 80% achieving parity with payment for medical benefits. The bill requires health plans that offer mental health coverage to have the same benefits, copayments and other treatment limits as other types of health care. This will allow more people with mental health disorders to receive treatment.

Although there been gradual improvement in this area in the last thirty eight years, through education and awareness campaigns by the psychiatric associations and other mental health organizations, much work still needs to be done to defeat the sigma attached to psychological problems. Mental illness is a chronic disease not a personal failing. Lawmakers and the lay public alike still need continued education.

****The Changing Role of the Psychiatrist****

When I was a young psychiatrist in the state hospital system the physician reined supreme. Within a few years, the psychiatrist's position started to erode. In 1974, although by title, I was still at the top of the medical totem pole at the mental health clinic, we were beginning to move toward a team model. On a daily basis, I had to explain my decisions and consider input from people who often were not as qualified or well trained. Patient care suffered as I spent more and more time filling out treatment plans and other documents needed by accrediting agencies and insurance companies.

At this juncture, my control over the doctor-patient relationship was also slipping. At Interact, for instance, when I was asked to give patient's injections of Prolixin, it was done in an assembly line fashion without my really knowing much about them, except for a quick look at their medical chart. I saw this as an ominous change foretelling the changing role of the psychiatrist from a clinician, who had a relationship with people, did therapy and also prescribed medication when appropriate, to a "pill pusher" and medication manager.

From there on, it seemed to me that we were on a slippery slide, where managed care, like the 1980's game "Pac Man," gobbled up more and more control over patient care. Psychologists and social workers moved up the ladder of control and were assigned to do therapy as patient care was split in half. The psychiatrist was delegated to do medication management and allowed 15 to 20 minutes with the patient. For many, prior authorization is required by their insurance companies to receive treatment or certain medications. This requires that the physician spend additional time on the phone or filling out forms and takes even more time away from therapeutic patient interaction. This is an inefficient system and probably does not save any money at all. Even though they are only doing a small part of the therapeutic process and have lost control of the treatment vehicle, <u>physicians still has full medical legal responsibility</u>. This is a frustrating dilemma.

An Integrated View of Treatment

Although there have been sweeping advances, during my career as a psychiatrist from 1967 to the present, there has also been a loss of the powerful therapeutic force that is the doctor-patient relationship. The focus of psychiatric treatment has gone from a Freudian model to an emphasis on physiologic mechanisms and brain chemistry. Its emphasis went from individual, group and family therapy to the more impersonal medication management. Even Frank J. Ayd Jr., M.D., known for his pioneering work in psychopharmacology, told TIME magazine in 1957, after the discovery of Thorazine, that drugs were "not a substitute for compassion, understanding, patience [or] an attentive ear." The mind and body act on each other in remarkable ways. As an Osteopathic physician, I feel that it is important to look at the whole person.

In spite of all the changes, the constant in my many years in the psychiatric profession has been my professional relationship with my patients. This is in direct contrast to what has been going on around me in the psychiatric community. I am a dinosaur. I do both medication management and therapy.

I was trained in the psychoanalytic approach in which the therapist is a blank silent screen upon which the patient projects his issues and develops transference. Therapy then was to deal with this transference, resistances and any counter transference issues that arose. I soon found that I was not comfortable being a silent therapist any more than I had been comfortable being a psychoanalytic patient in my training analysis with Dr. Isaac. Although I kept my psychoanalytic background as my core philosophy, I began talking more to my patient's and giving them more feedback. As the years went by, I added some aspects of cognitive behavioral therapy and even began to share disguised vignettes about my patients and my own life experiences. This gave me the chance to establish additional rapport and add the elements of education, reassurance and even at times humor. They seemed to appreciate it and often did well.

Doing therapy involves not only dealing with the patient's biological symptoms but also trying to understand and respond to the unique person within. This includes his/her background, frustrations, hopes, dreams and needs. Even with psychotic patients, it is often this human element that we deal with in therapy. Growing up with the patient again and understanding his/her trials, tribulations and traumas will allow the therapist to gain a perspective and help him/her mature and heal the child within. To be most useful, the therapist must also gradually understand him or herself and use this knowledge and the wisdom born of life experiences, as well as all his/her clinical and scientific information, to help the patient. My childhood and adolescent experiences made me a better, more empathetic and insightful psychiatrist.

Regardless of diagnosis, the patient and the psychiatrist are both human beings, or as Bella would say, "Human beans." The delicate balance between the biological basis of psychiatric illness, the uniqueness of the individual patient and the therapists' own life experiences are the three dimensions of understanding that a psychiatrist, like Perseus in Greek mythology, must constantly keep in view to be successful. These three things are the psychiatrist's best tools when doing therapy. They came into play the moment that I met Bella, took her hand and gently led her through the door of ward 3N. This balancing act has played out many times between my patients and me through the years. This is the dance with medusa that has occupied the core of my life in psychiatry.

ABOUT THE AUTHOR

H Michael Zal, D.O., F.A.C.N., F.A.P.A. has been a psychiatrist for over thirty-nine years. He is currently in private practice and a Clinical Professor in the Department of Psychiatry at the Philadelphia College of Osteopathic Medicine. He is board certified, a Fellow of American College of Neurology and Psychiatry and a Distinguished Life Fellow of the American Psychiatric Association.

Dr. Zal is a graduate of the University of Pennsylvania and the Philadelphia College of Osteopathic Medicine. He completed a three year Psychiatric Fellowship sponsored by the National Institute of Mental Health at the Philadelphia Mental Health Clinic and Haverford State Hospital.

He is Emeritus at the Belmont Center for Comprehensive Treatment and served as President of their Medical Staff. He was Chairman of the Psychiatric Service at Metropolitan Hospital in Philadelphia and a member of the University Of Pennsylvania Private Practice Research Group. He was also on the staff of Charter-Fairmount Institute, Mercy Suburban Hospital and the Medical College of Pennsylvania.

Dr. Zal received the Albert Einstein Healthcare Foundation Physicians' Award for Excellence and the Practitioner of the Year Award, from the Philadelphia Psychiatric Society, for outstanding character, dedication and commitment to patient care.

He is a lecturer, medical writer and editor on mental health topics with numerous published articles to his credit. He was the winner of the Eric W Martin Memorial Award, presented by the American Medical Writers Association, for outstanding writing and the Frances Larson Memorial Award for excellence. Dr. Zal is also the author of <u>Panic Disorder: The Great Pretender</u> and The <u>Sandwich Generation: Caught Between Growing Children and Aging Parents.</u> (Perseus Press).

Breinigsville, PA USA
25 April 2010

236750BV00001B/2/P